A Walk to the Crossroads

A WALK TO THE CROSSROADS

Friuli, Italy
2010

TOM PRESTON

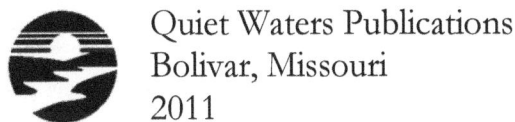

Quiet Waters Publications
Bolivar, Missouri
2011

Copyright ©2011 by Tom Preston. All rights reserved. No part of this book may be used or reproduced in any manner without written permission, except in the case of brief quotations embodied in critical articles and reviews.

For information contact:
Quiet Waters Publications
P.O. Box 34, Bolivar MO 65613-0034.
Email: QWP@usa.net.

For prices and order information visit:
    www.quietwaterspub.com

ISBN 978-1-931475-52-5 (UK edition)
Library of Congress Control Number: 2011909896

Cover photography and design: Andreas Hauch
Editor: Deborah Foss
Sketches: Karl Hartwig Kaltner.
Impressions of the area around the Dossaccio WW I Fortress, as well as landscapes around Trent and Friuli.
    www.kaltner-kh.com

Solvitur ambulando.
(It is solved by walking)

St. Augustine

Dedicated to Danny & Gernot,
Two friends
Who have journeyed with me in Europe
For over thirty years.

Contents

PROLOGUE TO ADVENTURE 9
SUBMARINES IN ITALY 13
DETOURS AND DISNEY..........................27
THE RED ROOSTER..................................39
THE OLD ROAD 61
FRANCESCO..73
TIMAVO AT THE CROSSROADS............87
AL CAVALLUCCIO 103
THE RILKE PATH..................................... 117
DIFFERENT EYES 127
ACKNOWLEDGEMENTS 135

Prologue to Adventure

As I left the house in Salzburg for the train station, I imagined Ghandi with his walking stick, taking long strides through India on his protest pilgrimage to the sea. Soon, I would be taking my own long strides with my own walking stick, though it would be on a different path to a different sea.

Just a day before, I had found the perfect walking stick in a nearby forest. My eleven-year-old son, Michael, had joined me on a short jaunt up the Felberbach in Aigen. It was a positive sign for me because I had been looking for a special walking stick ("Wanderstab", as we say), for years! As soon as I picked it up, Michael wanted it for himself. I told him it was too big for him, but the truth was that I had finally found my treasure after a long search. "This is my journey, Michi", I taunted, "and this little hummer's for me"!

The two of us had recently finished a two-week journey together, planning my walking tour through the wine country of Friuli to the sea. Our bond was strong and noticeable. Michael was going to spend a week with his friend's family in eastern Austria while I was away on my walking tour in Italy. *Va Bene!*

There was something thoughtful and gentle between us during our story time when he suddenly confessed, holding back his tears, that he had mixed emotions about staying with his friend's family for such a long time. I started to say something lame, like: "Stiff upper lip, buddy! Come, your brother and sister are gone that week too, and Mama has to work. You will be mega-alone the whole week if you stay here—and your friend will be disappointed".

Instead, I told him the story of being homesick on a four-day Mohave Desert Boy Scout Weekend when I was 12. "Yeah! I was homesick once, too", I extrapolated, fatherly, "but then I shared my homesick condition with my friend Bob. When he confessed that he was homesick just like me, well, then I wasn't homesick anymore"! I even tried adding some special wisdom, like "homesickness" meant that you had a home to begin with, a place to come home to that you miss when you are away—even if you are sometimes sick of it! However, that didn't really inspire him at the moment.

"Good try, Papa", he said, yawning. "Have a nice walk".

"Good night, Michael".

As I walked to the train station that day, the Ghandi image faded and instead, I thought about

A WALK TO THE CROSSROADS

Frodo's words to Gandalf about his uncle Bilbo in *The Lord of the Rings*:

> *He used often to say there was only one Road; that it was like a great river: its springs were at every doorstep and every path was its tributary. 'It's a dangerous business, Frodo, going out of your door', he used to say. 'You step into the Road, and if you don't keep your feet, there is no telling where you might be swept off to'*

Submarines in Italy

Many people spend their entire life indefinitely preparing to live.

Paul Tournier, *The Adventure Of Living*

It seemed from the very start that the old theme of "letting go" might just be the hidden agenda of my crazy adventure—walking for ten days through Italy. I had already abandoned the idea of trying to fit my Sony laptop into the large backpack. The moment I decided not to take it reminded me of an old cartoon I had once seen of a man walking across the desert. Every few hundred feet he discarded one thing after another, leaving behind all that was not of great value at the moment.

"It just flows better with the laptop", I had written to a friend in California, trying to convince myself I should bring it along. When writing by hand, I always ended up analyzing my handwriting, not being able to decipher my own shorthand inventions, whatsoever! It was like trying to read Esperanto backwards. If it didn't flow, I'd be stuck between my college writing style and my Austrian style—yet, I desperately wanted to begin writing! As I unpacked the laptop, I mused that the whole discussion in my head was like a Woody Allen movie!

An hour into the trip the following morning, I got stuck in a different way. The train from Salzburg to southern Austria had to pass through a transfer station in the higher Alps, where cars were loaded onto the trains for those who were prone to anxiety attacks when driving through the long tunnels. All of a sudden, the conductor's voice blared through the microphone, informing us that the locomotive had broken down. Its replacement would come in two hours; we would all have to wait. On top of that, it was pouring down rain!

"Oh shit"! was the most common phrase I heard in neighbouring compartments in the following minutes; a good phrase at appropriate times!

"I'll miss my connection"! was the second most used phrase.

Experienced traveller that I was, I reminisced about the dozens of times that such things had happened. Looking out the window at rain on the grass of the high meadows in Austria, I smiled and thought to myself: *It always works out. Often for the better! People start sharing sandwiches and passing around beers. You miss your boat but end up sleeping on the floor of some Italian harbour, meet some amazing people and exchange addresses—all because everyone was "stuck" and forced to let go of expectations.* I thought of Jack Johnson's song "Breakdown", when he longs for his "train" to have a breakdown—perhaps forcing him to slow down and bring about a new perspective on things.

I pulled a special book out of my backpack. *Love and War In the Apennine*s is a classic, a true story, which I had put off reading until that moment. At the onset of the story, the reader is plunged into World War II, as British and American spies are trying to pry their way into the German defences in Italy. The Fascists behind Mussolini had let Hitler in through the back door, and most of Italy was beginning to regret it!

The travel writer, Eric Newby, describes being in a submerged submarine near the coast of Sicily as its crew prepares for a secret mission to land on shore and sneak into the Nazi occupied airport. Their goal is to destroy as many bomber planes as possible. I've always had mixed feelings of excitement and fear when I think about being cooped up in a submarine under the sea. Then, at the very moment I read about (and physically felt) the crew's claustrophobia, as they were about to take a risky peek through the periscope—my fellow travellers and I realized that the climate-control in our train compartment was not functioning! No fresh air!

As the rain engulfed our abandoned train chain with no locomotive attached, someone recalled a train incident that had happened two weeks before. During a heat wave, a German self-encapsulated train (very modern!) lost its air-conditioning system, and no air was funnelling into the compartments whatsoever. People were literally fainting. Others panicked and tried to break the windows with hammers. Oddly enough, the train conductors seemed, at least at the onset, unconcerned about the problem. I was already feeling trapped without a heat wave, probably because the submarine story had "grabbed" me by the throat, so I quickly got up and looked around to see if the train doors were open. Thank God they were.

While I sucked in air at the door, laughing at my own "anxiety attack" and still waiting for the locomotive, a companion from my compartment started talking to me. He was a 75-year old farmer from Upper Austria.

"Just visiting a friend in Southern Austria", he said, trying to make some small talk. "I saw your big gnarly walking stick. Going hiking"?

"Ja"—just by myself", I told him in German. "I plan to walk through Italy for seven days, then dive into the ocean! Whatdaya think of that"?

Upon hearing the word "Italy" he announced proudly: "I never went to Italy and I never will"!

"Why's that"? I asked, truly surprised.

"My father fought against the Italians in the last war. He had nothin' good to say about 'em. Said they changed their colours midstream. Cowards! In the First World War they were neutral, then they had an alliance with Germany, then towards the end, with the Allies. In the Second World War they were first with Russia, then with the Fascists and Mussolini and…" he shook his head, flustered, "and then they changed their minds and tied in with the Allies".

"And what do *you* think about the Italians"? I asked, trying not to sound like a therapist, or as if I were talking to a young student.

"Oh, it's too late now" he chided, and "submerged", going back to work on his crossword puzzle.

There I was again—confronted with the wars! During my 40 years of living and travelling in Europe, I have never heard anyone say that they would not travel to Italy because the Italians had notoriously changed their minds.

Only recently had I felt the need to understand the First World War better, in order to understand the conflicts that still lie festering beneath the surface here in Austria, Slovenia and Italy. In addition, while exploring Western Slovenia and Friuli a while before the trip, I kept coming across memorials and information which I had never seen or heard of before. I found out later that communism had prevented the Slovenians from beginning to understand their recent history. Now that the Eastern Bloc countries are on their own, they are trying to work through the last 100 years by creating many new and impressive memorials and museums.

Researching the trails and rivers in preparation for my walking tour, I realized that the Slovenians and their Italian neighbours in that region have had conflicts over hundreds of years. My son and I had driven over the high pass between Traviso and northwest Slovenia a few weeks before, winding down into the upper Soča valley. Staying in Kobarid, even eleven-year-old Michael felt that something unique was going on. It was not only the beautiful Soča River, flowing deep and light blue in the gorge, inspiring poets and kayakers, that impressed him. There was a magnificent church and massive memorial, high on the hill overlooking the town.

This had been the place where some of the fiercest fighting had occurred. Hundreds of thousands had lost their lives in this small valley and in the high mountain passes, fighting for ideologies that only partly had to do with their lives; yet, they gave their lives for them! The Italians only wanted to gain control of Slovenian lands that bordered Italy! In the end, standing up to the Italians did help Slovenia to develop its own identity and a healthy patriotism. It was a mirror of how countries at war always deliver half-truths to its faithful soldiers (in this case, more so on the part of Italy) in order to meet their territorial, ideological or financial ends.

Michael and I also visited a museum in the older section of Kobarid, discovering that it was there that Hemingway served in the Red Cross as an ambulance driver during the worst fighting in the First World War. Out of that horrific experience came his book: *Farewell to Arms*, describing the many killings there in *Caporetto*, the Italian and English version of that town's name. It is revealing how Hemingway sees "Austria". He writes about the Austro-Hungarian Empire, which still existed at that time and shared its identity with Croats, Slovenians and Hungarians. They all fought under the same banner. Nowhere in Hemingway's book was the word "Slovenia" mentioned, though he wrote about a group of people called the "Slovenes". The sovereign country of Slovenia was not officially formed until 1991.

It is sad to think that the constant slaughter of soldiers and civilians occurred along the Isonzo River during World War I because Italy wanted to control the entire Dalmatian Coast (including the harbour at Trieste) and because the Austrian monarchy wanted to keep its empire together. Austria, however, tried to develop the Slavic countries more than is often realized by establishing a Slovenian university in Trieste, which had a large Slovenian population.

These Isonzo battles made the conflict during the Civil War in the States look like child's play! Over a period of two years, the Italian and Austrian conflict along the Isonzo River cost the lives of 1.2 million soldiers. The Civil War in the States, all toll: 600,000 killed!

As they finally hooked up the locomotive and readied the train to wind through the Alps into Italy, I thought about the real reason Italy went to war. Psychologically speaking, it was to strengthen its identity as a country. The socialists were against the war. The fascists wanted to control the Mediterranean and demonstrate their new identity, like adolescents trying to prove their masculinity.

I told my son about Vietnam, and how the United States government told us that we must fight there to keep communism from spreading all over the eastern world. Then I described the tens of thousands of young boys who were slaughtered and mutilated for an ideology which did not really have a solid backbone, filled with half-truths. I told him that the fighting there in Kobarid was similar.

A WALK TO THE CROSSROADS / 21

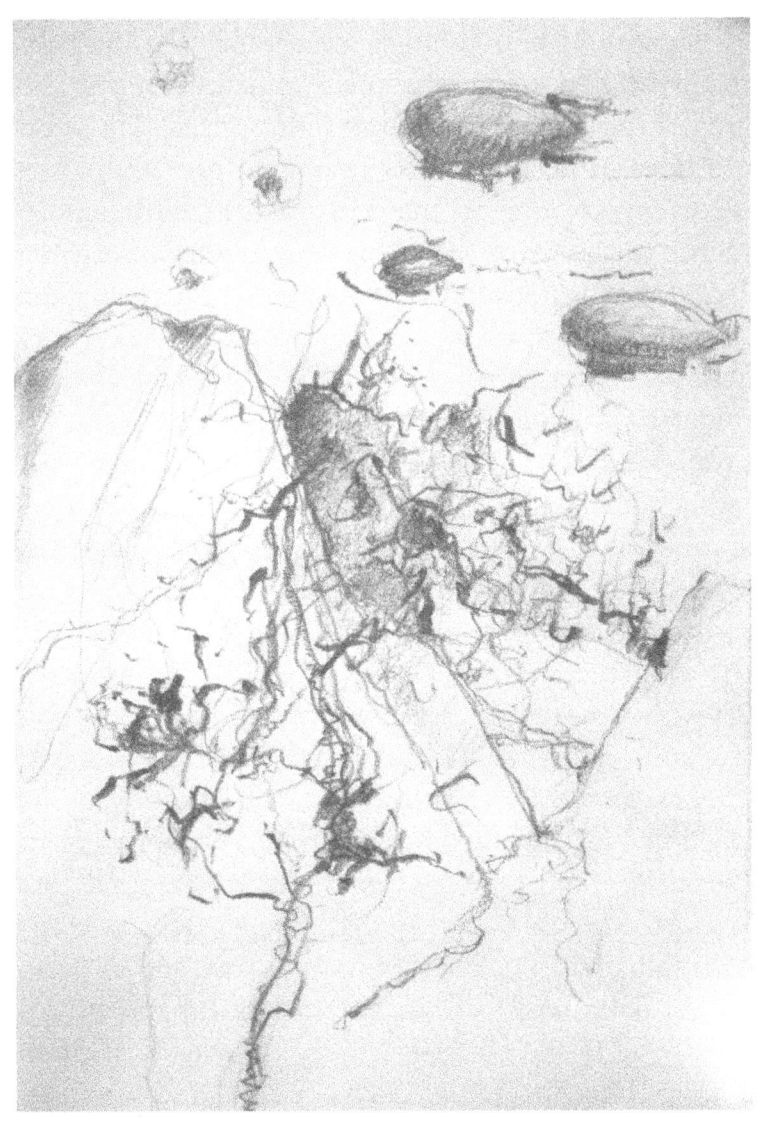

I also told him about George Bush and the half-truths he told a few years back, when attempting to bolster the American spirit to fight in Iraq. The good old boys protecting "God and apple pie" and CNN media hype came to mind, as well as naïve young men trying to earn their "brownie points", believing 100% that they were keeping the world clean (and perhaps Americanized) for democracy. The story kept getting closer to us. I think Michael might have understood what George Bush didn't: the reality of lower class boys duped by the media into joining the military and fighting in Iraq. "It's a bit like peer pressure in school", I wanted to say, "when a few in the class convince the rest to join in".

I did not even want to bring up the reasons why the United States entered into WWI with Michael. As with all wars, the reasons were and are too dubious and ridiculous to talk about, even 95 years later.

The train started with a sudden jolt, knocking my walking stick out of the rack above. With a wink to the farmer and his crossword puzzle, I mused that Italy was the only country that entered the war by its own initiative. The Italians wanted land and clout in the Adriatic, and had an attitude of superiority towards the Slavic countries. They believed that these countries needed guidance and cultural development. The soup was getting hot because Germany wanted to be more of a big shot and drew Austro-Hungary into the war to keep the "Slavic folk" under their wings. The Slovenian population, far from having its own identity, was caught in the middle, needing to be loyal to the Austrian monarchy, but seeing, at the same time, that they were somewhat a pawn in someone else's game.

Italy wanted to possess the harbour in Trieste, and many Italian speaking and thinking residents of Trieste did not want to be a pawn of the Austrian monarchy any longer. It was time for the monarchies to dissolve, as most knew. Italy wanted more of the good wine country that is now Slovenia, as well as the bilingual area in South Tirol. Italy was briefly aligned with the Triple Alliance (Germany, Austria-Hungary, Italy) for a while. In the end, Italy officially entered the war on the side of the Allies and finally gained victory, not over the Dalmatian coast, but of the harbour in Trieste. My farmer companion was somewhat right about the opinion-changing Italians!

Italy and Slovenia: These were the countries I was heading for – now that the locomotive was in gear. The old farmer from Upper Austria brought up age-old questions, without knowing it! The questions were: Why do we listen to the half-truths of our fathers and mothers, especially about war? Because we love and trust our parents! Why do we listen to the half-truths of our country's government? Because we are sometimes cowards ourselves! We submerge like submarines in our fears and comfort zones. We fear that if we really begin to live as we should live, and hear and see the truth as it really is, that it might become a bit uncomfortable. It might make us real and different, and who wants to be real or different?

Detours and Disney

*The path to the center is never straight
but always clear.*

Gernot Candolini, *Labyrinths, Walking Toward The Center*

Sometime back in the seventies, when I was travelling around the world, stumbling into wine cellars in Jerusalem, or finding myself alone in Peshawar, Pakistan, I learned that detours and mistakes on our journeys do not necessarily have to be disasters or a waste of time.

After taking the train over the Alps and travelling by bus to Cividale, I finally set out on my walking tour through northern Italy. Donning my backpack, I grabbed my huge walking stick and just took off in the direction I had originally planned to take. I should have studied the map better. Plotting out the route with my son a while back, we had focused on the area south of Cividale. I just figured that the quaint, back-road path merged with another that would guide my feet into the vineyards south of town. I have a fairly good sense of direction—or so I thought!

I was so eager to set off, I did not notice that I was taking the road back to Slovenia! The irony of it is that this route would have taken me back to Caporetto, where I originally wanted to start the tour. My plan had been to wind down the Soča Valley and trace the Soča River to the sea. As it enters Italy, the river's name changes to "Isonzo". For several reasons I had abandoned that plan and now here I was, already walking two kilometres in the wrong direction! In the end, I was rewarded for my dumb-detour mistake. I turned right and followed a beautiful farm path that led me into a gentle circle alongside cornfields and vineyards. It wound back through old town Cividale, stumbling upon the Natisone River, which runs through this once powerful town just north of the old Roman town of Aquileia. As I studied a second map, I realized that the Natisone River actually has its source in the mountains this side of Caporetto, which have formed the language barrier that has divided Slovenia and Italy for over a thousand years. It was as if this old river was tapping me on the shoulder, saying: "You nerd! Not only are you doing something you had decided against, but you almost missed the beauty of the fields and the river as it flows through old Cividale"!

It was an unexpected detour—and an unexpected blessing.

Back on the right road, I wandered through the growing number of vineyards of the southeastern part of Friuli. The proper name of the region, by the way, is *Friuli-Venezia Giulia.* Two things became evident as I found the rhythm in my steps, letting the walking stick support me as I walked along the road. First, everyone else was moving much faster, obviously. Reality set in as bikers, cars and tractors consciously slowed in order to manoeuvre around me. Second, I loved the feeling that the walking stick gave me as it propelled me along with earthy turbo energy. It was great fun and no real burden, either.

In fact, it became little joke between me and the fields, as I finally had time to watch the flowers, birds and streams go by, taking stock of them at the pace I wished to take at that moment! What a privilege! What a treasure-chest full of pearls and gems! I'd often take a side road just to lie down and listen to a stream going by, or walk between the rows of the vineyards, snatching a few grapes. Because the climate is much warmer in Italy, the grapes would be ready for harvest a month earlier than in Austria. When I popped the grapes into my mouth, they were already very sweet in mid-August.

It was already late in the afternoon and I needed to make a choice between two roads up ahead, in order to find one of the B&B farmhouses I had seen a month earlier. On the right hand side of the street there suddenly appeared a simple wine tasting house that seemed to be beaconing to me. I convinced myself (it did not take me long) that it was time for a rest. As I propped up the backpack at an outside table, setting my walking stick along the side wall of the old farmhouse, I thought of Frodo's words to Pippen about "the dangers of taking shortcuts to pubs", especially because I had not yet nailed down my B&B, and the thunderclouds were quickly building over the Slovenian Alps. I risked it, however, and it was good that I did!

Their own wine, a perfectly chilled Sauvignon Blanc, served with huge green olives and homemade cheese, tasted like a king's feast after three hours of walking in the fresh air. Breakfast already seemed like light years ago. Besides that, the woman serving gave me some helpful hints. She told me that a few of the B&Bs were closed, but suggested three possibilities just a few kilometres up the road—two of them up a steep hill, the other in the valley. *"Avanti! Avanti!* Get thee be gone, lad", she prompted. "A storm might be a brewin'"!

Realizing that she was younger than I and had called me "lad", made me smile. I thanked her and was off again—almost forgetting the walking stick leaning on the wooden siding of the farmhouse. The clouds, wind and sun were forming beautiful patterns on the vineyards and hillsides. I marvelled at how every thirty meters the landscape seemed to change. In a car, one doesn't notice these small nuances. I had ignored the threat of the coming storm because it created such a light show on the light green and subtly brown fields. However, the thunder was rolling and I had to do something! Duck under a bridge? Dash into a barn? Use my magic stick like Moses to calm the tempest?

At that moment, I gazed up at the upcoming junction. Hanging at all sorts of angles were signs that pointed to three or four famous places up on the hill, two of them B&Bs. This fit my original expectation. I dreamed of finding a place on a hill next to an old café, nestled close to an old church, where I could do some writing and reading for half the day—and later, test out the local wines.

When a lightning bolt flashed in the next valley, I turned around and watched when, in front of my nose, a large van swerved, almost hitting me. The driver was just checking out the weather before driving off again. I hailed him down and asked him if he could give me some advice. *"Scusi, Signore"*, I began, "Do you know much about the places up the hill"?

"Un pò", he replied. "I used to live near here". He thought for a moment, observing me carefully from head to foot and said: "Come on! The storm is coming. I'll drive you up"!

My idealism struggled with neediness. I had set a goal of travelling every step by foot, and here I was, faced with the decision of giving up my goal on the very first day of the walking tour! Then I thought (in between the second and third thunderclap) *Why not?* And blurted out: "Mille Grazie! Andiamo Capitano"!

He winked at me and said: "I might even have room for your 'shepherds cane'", as he called it.

Once up the hill, we checked out many choice spots but discovered that they were all closed or, in some cases, the owners were doing some renovation. (Why didn't they write this on the signs below?) The last place on top of the hill would have been Castelmonte, a few kilometres ahead. I was calculating how long it would take me to walk back down and said: "Well, let's try one more option". I was beginning to feel a bit guilty about all his efforts.

"Things have changed", he nodded. "These small farmers always used to keep their places open. Now they take vacations at the end of August, too"!

I slipped him the piece of a napkin upon which an address and a hastily scribbled map was written. The woman at the wine tasting house did not have any decent paper. He looked at the paper, laughed and said, "Did she write it on a piece of toilet paper"? Then, *"Ah! Sì,* I know this place! It's in the village of Spessa! I used to do business with the previous owner. Good place"!

I was a bit relieved, to say the least. The lightning and thunder kept up, but the rain never came. The air was very tense. As we drove back down the long hill, he started talking quickly, as if I understood every word. He told me that he was 75 and still farming.

"No, Signore"! I insisted. *"Non è possibile!* You're not that old"!

"Sì, sì"! He said, winking at me. He talked about his kids who had all attended college. One was even studying "Disney Animation".

"Really"? I was genuinely surprised, of course.

"*Si! È possibile.* In Florence! It's a special graphic arts training degree, enabling him to work on Disney animation projects in Italy", he said proudly.

While we wound down the mountain and then up the valley again, I mentioned that my father had been a graphic artist with Disney in Hollywood before the war. "He worked on *Fantasia*—you know—drawing many pictures of Mickey Mouse bailing water to hold back the flood that he had set in motion". I was wondering if the same thing would happen to us if this storm finally let loose with full strength, when he suddenly laughed out loud: *"Ah, fantastico! Fantasia* was the first animated film I saw after the war. We had no money, but our uncle from Venice came up and invited us all to the cinema"!

As he turned up the long path leading to the wine farmer's small estate in Spessa (without needing the directions written on the napkin), the sun came out! A young, roundish woman greeted us and asked what we were looking for. The old farmer next to me returned the greeting and told her that I needed a room. She looked me over a few seconds then said: *"Si, certo"!* The farmer's wife told me the price was forty euros a night, then asked me to wait.

I climbed out of his van, and remembering my "pasturing cane" (a magic wand, "like Mickey, you know"? he had jested!), thanked the old farmer. "Say hello to your Disney student for me", I yelled.

"Okay! Ciao"!

It was an unexpected detour—with one more unexpected blessing!

Irene and André seemed standoffish at first sight. He was welding something in the garage while she showed me the room around the back and upstairs. It was very modern, as the old farmhouse had been newly renovated. I asked right away if there was a local osteria or restaurant nearby, so that I could walk there later and grab something to eat. During my long talk with the "Disney farmer", as I called him afterwards, I had not realized how far into the country we had driven; I still was not used to being without a car.

"*Sì!* There is a restaurant three kilometres from here", she said slowly, realizing that I was on foot.

"Nothing nearer"? I pressed.

"No, sorry".

After I put away a few things and took off my hiking boots, she came in and offered: "You can eat with us, if you want—a simple meal. We will eat in two hours when the work is finished. My husband and I need to use the last hours of light today", she said in perfect English.

"Mille Grazie" I said solidly, feeling at the same time oddly in their debt.

I gazed out the windows at the beautiful vineyards. I even stuffed a pipe, walked down on the west side of the vineyard to what I later found out was the Merlot section and smoked a bit. André and his younger brother were doing some work in between the rows of grapevines, their branches heavy with red and white grapes. The storm that had threatened us all had petered out somehow and the sun was caressing the leaves and my hair.

As we dined that night—and the word is not superficially chosen—I learned that they were both learned vintners and both spoke excellent English. They were even organic-wine farmers. Everything they produced, from wine to pigs, was handled without the use of chemicals or pesticides. Irene had prepared some homemade polenta from organically-grown corn, sausages from their own pigs, salad from their garden, homemade cheese pancakes with wheat they grew themselves, topped off with the first Merlot they had produced after five years of hard work! How on earth did I earn all this?

Irene and André took some time to fill me in on the agriturismo farms in the area. Hundreds of small wine farmers had gone into "agri's", as they called them, offering B&Bs to supplement their income. It was also a heart-felt way to keep in contact with people, make their own wines known to others in Europe and bring in some money to renovate the very old farmhouses that were inherited from great grandfathers and grandmothers!

"We are basically closed now, as many are at the end of August. We only have guests from April to mid-August", Irene said.

"So why did you make an exception with me"? I asked, a bit cheeky after the third Merlot.

Irine said dryly: "I just liked you. I trust my intuition"!

I had to laugh—and thanked them again.

They told me a bit about the histories of their families and why they had chosen to become grape farmers. She was the daughter of a butcher and had studied English at the university. He was an engineer and a jack-of-all-trades. They had just decided to take a risk and learn by doing—and here they were—grape farmers with chickens, pigs and fresh air! At the end of the evening, they looked at the map I had pasted into my nifty spiral notebook, moving their fingers carefully along the small roads I had enlarged of the area.

"Keep along this path and you will have more shade and less traffic… and more beauty", suggested André.

"There are more opportunities to take small farm roads if you go this way", added Irene. "If you get this far along the Collio, you may slip into Slovenia and spend the night at the place where we celebrated our wedding"!

I had asked too many questions and was too tired to ask one more. What was the deal with this "Collio" that I kept reading and hearing about? This was one question that was left unanswered that evening. I bade them goodnight and went up to look at the stars over the vineyards. A nice full moon would be rising in a few days.

In Disney's film, *Fantasia*, the magician's nephew learned how to use his "magic stick" wisely. He made a few mistakes along the way, causing a flood because he was too curious and did not follow the rules. My small but adventuresome detours did not destroy or deemphasize that which my walking tour was all about. Among other things, the detours were the spice! No, even more—they were the unintended backbone of the tour! Ha!

Unexpected detours—and unexpected blessings!

The Red Rooster

If you haven't grasped it with your hands,
You can't comprehend it.
If you don't go there with your feet,
You can't understand it.

Gernot Candolini, *Labyrinths: Walking Toward The Center*

The goal I had set for myself on my walking tour was more or less to cover seven to ten kilometres each day and then relax, write and smoke my pipe in the late afternoons and evenings. Yesterday I had been graciously granted ample cloud cover, which protected me from the heat of the sun.

The afternoons were usually pretty hot this time of the year, but the weather had been just right for the first steps: cloudy, a light wind and impending storms.

The next day, however, promised to be different. I felt it when I awoke. Staying the night on a farm often means (all over the world!) that a rooster is somewhere in the vicinity. Even in up-to-date 2010, with modern winemaking equipment and technology to regulate the crops and keep up on the market in They put us up competitive Tuscany—even then—the rooster will let off some prophetic steam at around 6 a.m. I couldn't help inadvertently thinking back to one morning in the fall of 1973 when I was stuck in the country suburbs of Istanbul.

I was flying from Kabul, Afghanistan, to London, already battling dysentery, which caused me to leave the country sooner than planned. Ariana Airlines had bought a few old DC8s from the 1960s and they probably needed overhauling. As we took off, the pilot told us in English that we would have to land again due to a loose screw in the cockpit. (No joke!) An hour after we took off the second time, we had a *déjà vu* experience. The pilot spoke again through the microphone: "Ladies and Gentlemen, we have a small fire in one of the engines. We will have to land in Istanbul and spend the night".

I was young and did not have a lot of stressful plans in my datebook. No big deal. When I fly I usually just pray that if we have to go down, then please over water and not over the suburbs of Newark, New Jersey!

They put us up in an old hotel near a farm. Low and behold, after four hours of counting (Turkish) sheep—the rooster did his duty—and loud! I was trying to figure out whether the roosters there sounded different than the few I had experienced in La Canada, where I grew up in Southern California. Sure, I had been on my uncle's farm in Ohio—one gets a bit of "rooster experience" somehow in life—but this was too much! This rooster didn't want to stop either! He probably was suffering from the noise of the planes—being "roostered-up" near the airport—or maybe the stress of the air traffic was ruining his sex life!

So, as I yawned and stretched in Italy that morning, wondering if I should get up with the early birds, my personal Italian rooster went off, sort of like Old Faithful in Yellowstone. "I'm here", he cock-a-doodle-dooed"! Thank God he did not doodle around as long as that bird in Istanbul.

As he continued to exercise his masculine, show-off throatiness (not unlike a lot of Italian machos I meet!) my Swatch told me it was 6:14 a.m. (could be worse!). I looked briefly out the window. The sun was already saying: *You're gonna feel me today, buster! You can bet your bottom dollar on it!* It was going to be a hot one.

I was the only guest at the bed & breakfast farmhouse, which meant that I had most of the breakfast spread to myself. André's brother shared the feast; he was as hungry as I, after all his work in the vineyard the day before. There was Müesli, homemade yoghurt and homemade apple strudel—even a modern espresso machine! So, I was not really suffering; in fact, I have seldom seen such a breakfast! Good start!

Irene reminded me, however, that many of the B&Bs were closed during the "Ferro Augusto", the Italian hot-spell-vacation time at the end of August. It was hard to find out on the Internet how many of the *agriturismo* farms were open or not. I had thought that this might be the case, but I also had figured that many would want to profit from city-dwellers who came to the wine country to cool off and enjoy Friuli. No bananas! I had enough ideas and suggestions from Irene and André, however, to make some walking plans that worked for me that day.

Saying farewell to this unusually helpful couple, I headed down the long dirt driveway leading away from the wine (and pig!) farm in Spessa, and let the morning sun stroke my skin. The fields were still holding a bit of dew from the night, and I loved every step of it! The vineyards, small cliffs and clusters of trees provided a feast for my senses and occasional shade for my head. Soon, however, that which I was looking for somewhat unconsciously, came to

A WALK TO THE CROSSROADS / 43

me more quickly than I expected: I was about to begin an early morning crash course in *"Friuli vino cultura"* and its history as I walked though the various zones and valleys of a most famous wine area.

After an hour of shady walking, I realized that I had taken (as I often did) an alternate route between the hills. However, I ended up in the same place I had intended to go in the first place. Maybe I just don't really like following directions—it's too boring! It doesn't allow for surprises! I rested my oversized but steady and faithful walking stick on an oak tree and read the map. I realized that I had already circled Prepotto and was walking in a small inland valley along the Judrio River.

I walked further towards the south and came across a very large information board. It described the whole valley, the villages and the special wine that grows there. Apparently, the weather, earth and wind conditions create a climate that is ideal for growing the grapes of special red and white wines called "Schiopetto". Winemaker Mario Schiopetto was one of the first to incorporate German wine-making techniques, like cold fermentation, into white wine production in the Collio. It became a nice specialty of the area.

The long and narrow valley is recognized by wine specialists today (and by villagers who have lived there for over a thousand years) as a special zone. The Judrio flows quietly through this valley, which is about six kilometres long and three kilometres wide, sandwiched between Slovenian vineyards on the east side and a small ridge on the Italian west side.

I could hear the Judrio River talking to me on the left side of the road, hidden between the trees. It couldn't fool me, though. Seemingly small and unimportant, it gently waters and refreshes this valley, then flows into the farmlands between the Torre and Isonzo Rivers where it forms a lake. The clever Judrio River trickles out of the lake underground and empties into the Adriatic Sea. Rivers have personalities, always, but we seldom notice them.

As I studied the map once again, taking a rest near the village of Dolegna, I had to chuckle to myself. I realized that the Judrio has its source way up in the mountains next to that convent on the hill in Castelmonte where I almost went the day before. It was as if the rivers were constantly showing me the way! The Judrio's source taunted me: "Not up here, silly, but down there, where the wine is good and the path leads to the sea. *Si! Benissimo*"!

The fascinating part of this journey was that I was the only person I met for days; in fact, I never met anyone who was doing what I was doing! One drives a car to pick up something at the market or rushes to make the traffic light over the Judrio Bridge to get home in time for the start of the soccer game. I did not find anyone, however, who just walked along the Judrio for three hours like I did, listening to its whispering and to my faithful walking stick as it hit the dirt, bonding me to the earth a little bit more. Cars went rushing by. On the smaller roads, tractors rumbled past. Bikers rushed by, working on their haemorrhoids by the minute, not really looking content. I had all the time in the world just to walk step-by-step, through this wonderful part of God's good earth. I was in heaven, just walking.

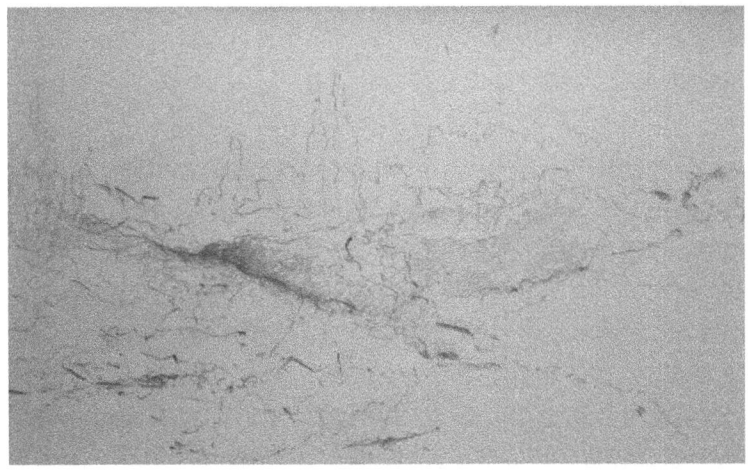

I would read historic signs and occasional *"Informazione sul Friuli Storico"* about wines and villages and the names of wine farmers. It was a privilege to walk along the vineyards, streets and hills—smelling the earth, touching it and picking sweet grapes of all sorts. These grapes would be used to make wines that soon would find their way to the tables of the most knowledgeable wine lovers in the world. That was awesome! Awesome, perhaps in a different way than kids in the States have used the word since the 1970s. I would put the emphasis on being truly in "awe" of the basics that quiet the centre of my being—so much, that my mouth opens wide with respect!

A week later, after I had reached the saltwater of the Adriatic, I tasted wines with Marino, the owner of the restaurant where I was staying. He raved about this and that wine from this or that valley and let me smell the differences between them—as if he knew the earth and had played on that ground as a kid.

I couldn't hold back. *"Si, capisco, Marino"*, I said laughing. "I just walked through that village a week ago! I can imagine what you're talking about. I think I stopped at that field and took a short rest, smoked a pipe, knocked the mud from my shoes, walked in between the rows of grapes, or drank out of the stream nearby! I smelled it! I often wondered why the grapes of certain wines grow in hilly areas, whereas others grow in the flatlands".

Parts of that morning's journey were boring, as well. A few bad streets challenged my patience. A bicyclist and a tractor almost ran me off the road, my backpack and I landing in a cornfield. Pebbles slipped into my hiking boots. Flies crawled around on my face. A small, ugly industrial area, built to boost the economy in the Judrio Valley, came into view. (Not all wine farmers have a good income.)

A WALK TO THE CROSSROADS / 47

At one point I took a detour through a vineyard, thinking the road would cross the Judrio on the adjacent side. The area was breathtaking, with ornate groves of rush, ferns and phallic looking pods—all lining the cornfields and vineyards—but I soon realized that there was no bridge! Crossing the river would mean wading through it up to my knees. The small Judrio became bigger when I did not expect it—as if it had its own personality and wanted to play a dirty trick on me! I doubled back, listening to the Judrio River talking to the trees, trying not to be ticked off that I was covering the same ground.

A few things stood out that morning. On the side of the road there was always a mixture of seven or eight types of wildflowers and grasses. No matter where I walked, on the street or on small, gutted farm roads, nature's wonders were present. The contrast of vegetation along the roadsides in Austria is less amazing, where perhaps two or three varieties of weeds and wildflowers grow. Here, however, there was an orgy of wildflowers by the road—a competition to see how many exquisite flowers, weeds and grasses could reproduce and grow together within one hundred meters! I stuck my giant walking stick into the flowers occasionally, just to keep my balance, keep me grounded, or to keep from being hit by a cyclist!

Further, I started feeling the crass difference between driving and walking. This was nothing new, of course; I was a backpacker throughout the Sierras and the Alps in my younger years. This contrast, however, seemed to take on new dimensions on my walking tour. The cars would pass me and arrive at the destination where I was heading in around five minutes—while I needed an hour on foot! Such experiences sort of fry your brain. Expressed more poetically, I was able to feel time and earth differently. When the landscape changes ever so slowly, one has the feeling that each curve is another world, another personality. In the car one sees the changes as if in a film. Walking, one senses four or five gradual changes as nature bends and is transformed with splendid and subtle differences.

Eventually it was time to start looking for my lodging. At the next junction I took a northeastern route heading towards Slovenia. On a hill to my left was an old *castello* (castle) and *weingut* as we say in German, the word for a large wine estate. To the right was an old pub on the side of the road. That looked splendid! I sat in the midday sun taking in the simplicity and drank a beer—or two. Reading the last few chapters of my book, I just let the time go by.

My goal that day was to climb another hill towards the village of Plessiva in Slovenia. I hoisted my backpack again, said goodbye to the beer mug(s), grabbed my walking stick and headed up the road again. After one kilometre, I reached the beautiful

Plessiva Nature Park, but had to walk up a long winding hill to find the village.

On the ridge, the sun was coming on strong. I was on the top of a ridge and tried to decide which way to go. I recognized the place I had checked out a few weeks earlier with my son. To the right were the nice church, an earthy café and a B&B. To the left, was a sign pointing to a B&B in Plessiva, just over the border. As I trudged across the old border into Slovenia (thinking about the fact that it was not too long ago that I needed a passport to do so!) I sensed stillness in the air. It was siesta time. Besides that, the B&B was closed! Darn it! Back we go to Italy, a kilometre to the south! *Ah, there is a nice B&B*, I said to myself, viewing a farm on the left that overlooked a large valley. Then, the sober news—*Chiuso*—it was closed, as well!

I talked to a few people in the village and most said to keep on the road to Cormons. I was torn because I wanted to be on this hillside, enjoying the view! That was my goal! The wind was blowing lightly, but I felt the sun on my head. I had been walking for almost five hours. If I had to walk down into Cormons to find lodging it would take another two hours, and the lodging would be more expensive. I had to make a decision. I had a lot of energy, but I knew that it wasn't good to push it when the sun was so strong. After all, I wasn't 29 anymore!

I took a long swig of water and then headed downhill towards the southeast on the road to Cormons. I popped several grapes into my mouth along that path (don't tell anyone). The road to the village where Irene and André had been married was four kilometres off towards the north, further into Slovenia. It just did not seem right to take that route. How does one make such decisions? The big ones—and the little ones?

By this time I was right smack dab in the middle of the Collio! I had seen the word all over, used in many ways. What was it? A mountain? A large town? It was finally explained as I stood in the shade of a small rural intersection in the first village on the way towards Cormons. A large historical board showed in a cartoon image the whole area I had been walking through. It pointed out with a yellow dot that I was standing in the middle of an historic winegrowing region called *Collio*—the most prestigious wine area in Friuli-Venezia Giulia. It's like Napa Valley in northern California. Resting between Cividale in the flatlands to the west, the Adriatic coast to the south, Gorizia and the Isonzo to the East and the Slovenian Alps to the north, the name "Collio" is taken from the Italian word "Colli" which means "hillside". I read further in German and Italian:

> *These hills are endowed with a unique microclimate, where strong winter winds, such as the "Bora", along with gentle*

A WALK TO THE CROSSROADS / 51

summer breezes, spring rains and sunny days, live in harmony together, creating a proper climate for famous wines which have been recorded since Roman times. More definitely, in the year 1300, the Ribolla Gialla wine was already well known, grown across the Isonzo River from Gorizia.

OK, nice hype! I thought. They have to describe it in flowery tones. The whole area puts out money for solid advertising! Standing with my walking stick and backpack, I wasn't in the mood to enter into the Collio's history. I needed to get going; the sun was baking my ears off even when standing in the shade! I could use a little of that Bora wind!

On the map there were seven villages on the way down to Cormons. One of them would surely let this straggling wine-noviciate into their household. The first one looked fantastic, the kind of place where one would like to stay for a week! However, obviously everybody had thought the same as I, as the place was full. The next three villages had no B&Bs, and the final three were a few kilometres up on a hill out of walking reach.

As I walked over the last crest before winding down into the famous wine centre, Cormons, a beautiful church on the left provided some shade. A thought came to me, one I often had in this area: The churches and the café culture were not as cosy as in other parts of Italy. There was a kind of "coldness" about them, a definite influence of the more sober Slovenian culture. Was I just used to Tuscany?

As I wound down to the outskirts of Cormons, I was getting a bit desperate. To the right I noticed a sign on an old artsy type house: *"Camere"* (rooms). Oh, that is a good sign, I thought, as I knocked on the door.

A woman came out and said: "No, I do not let rooms out anymore…" (Why the sign, then?) "But I know of two possibilities. First…" as she pointed away from Cormons to a small town to the east, "you take that road over there. Follow it for one kilometre to Pradis. Then you will find a sign: *La Gallo Rosso*, she mimicked with her hands and voice, *Kiki kiri*, like a rooster—and *rosso*, like your red headband"!

The name of the second place was too hard to remember, but it was just around the bend from the first one, so I jetted off with my walking stick once again through the vineyards. It was still very hot at 4 p.m. in August—without the Bora wind! I had been walking with my backpack for six hours, less the beer-stop!

After half an hour, I finally spotted 30 to 40 cars in front of the next entrance. "What are so many cars doing here out in the country"? I asked myself out loud. As I drew near, I realized that they all had followed the red sign made out of wood at the bottom of the path leading up to the wine farmer's house. The sign showed a red rooster with the words: "Gallo Rosso".

"That's it"! I exclaimed again too loud, doubting a bit. What was everyone doing here? A wine tasting party? New opening? Was it perhaps the only place to stay for miles and so there were no vacancies? I believed it! Were my chances looking slimmer each minute?

Sweat dripped down my face, backpack and shirt; with walking stick in hand, I moved between well-dressed people looking for the person in charge. The signora came over and I tactfully blurted out: "I need a room desperately. Is there one free"?

"No", she replied, subdued, but polite. "We have had a death in the family and they have just returned from the funeral".

All the funeral guests glared at me while they prepared to eat something together with their community. They did not know that I was a pastor and used to performing funerals. It was a bit odd and embarrassing, standing there with red bandana, hiking shoes and walking stick. The woman kindly suggested, "Try the house down the road a bit. It's called *Casa Mafalda*". I retained the name somehow and left as unobtrusively as possible, taking the way I came, wondering what would come next.

As I wound my way up the dirt road to Casa Mafalda, I was already determined to throw myself under the huge tree in front of the house and drink the water from the dish of the German shepherd chained up there, if need be. At that moment a woman rode up on her bike and asked me: "Hey, what are you looking for"?

"For a room, what else"? I asked, nervously looking over at the dog yanking at his chain.

"Oh great! We are open all year", she boasted, revealing that she spoke English pretty well. "Two rooms are free"!

"The best news I've heard all day", I said. "I'll take one"!

She introduced herself as Maurizia and said that she had been an au pair in the States when she was 19. "Yeah, then I married a wine farmer and have been here ever since! Come on. I'll show you your room! Then you can come down, sit in the shade and relax a bit under the oak tree"! (Had she read my thoughts?)

It was great just to sit after seven hours of walking (minus two beers and putting my ears to the fields to hear the river). In sandals, shorts and a fresh shirt, I drank some water and chatted with Maurizia.

"Don't worry about the German shepherd. He's too old to bite anyone".

She shared about the wine estate, about renovating the old house and about the time she spent in the States, 27 years ago. She did not look 46, but her two sons proved it when they rolled up the dirt road.

"Hey, how about a glass of your own wine, chilled a bit"? I asked politely, but thirsty and curious. Maurizia pulled out two bottles of their wine—chilled perfectly—without labels, but good! Oh Lord, I knew I had found the right place, somehow! We ended up finishing off both bottles—okay, one was half empty already—and Maurizia felt like talking. She said I was a bit crazy to be walking around alone for a week with my dumb walking stick. When I told her that I was a Lutheran pastor, she almost rolled off the chair with laughter!

Well into the second bottle she asked me: "How can you believe in God when all these disasters happen"? She knew it would then get heavy and threw a bone to the other smaller and more neurotic dog that had just appeared on the scene. Maurizia started talking about her husband, who was attending the funeral at the Red Rooster. "He is not taking the funeral very well. The man who died was a leading figure in the town. He was an older role model, a father figure for many men over the last 30 years. It has hit my husband really hard". Then she said: "My husband is 20 years older than I am. That hits me hard, too. A lot of things are new to him these days—I need to work three days a week taking care of a 90-year old woman to make ends meet, and he also has to take care of fixing breakfast for the guests. Wine farmers in his generation just didn't do things like that"!

My wine education was expanded further, as well. She talked about the types of wine they made and let me know about the "Tocai" story, a big thing for them! The Hungarians had developed this variety of grape over the last hundred years, developing a sweeter dessert wine and naming it *Tokaj*. The Italians drank *Tocai* for hundreds of years, but it was the dry wine from the Collio! Just a year ago, however, they passed a law in Friuli (after heated EU discussions!) that this same grape varietal should be called Friulano in Italy. It was an identity thing, but it also had to do with wine culture, history, and truth! They were a bit proud of the new development. (But they still call it both: *Tocai* and *Friulano*.)

Maurizia also let me know about her love/hate relationship with the Slovenians. "I don't like their language"! she frowned. "I mean, when Fred Flintstone comes on TV and they translate Wilma as saying: '*Dobrodošel doma, moj najljubši vrabec, Fred—welcome home, my darling sparrow.*' It just doesn't fit". She laughed, and then said: "Two different cultures and languages so close to each other is not always easy—anywhere—anytime. It goes deep. Old war wounds. Old animosities from over 900 years—not just 90"!

She reminded me that the Collio has two parts; on the map one mostly sees the Italian Collio, but the Slovenian Collio is just as big. It lies behind the Italian Collio and is called *"Goriska Brda"*, in Slovenian. Their wines were also good. "The earth is the same and the wind is the same, although they are a bit higher in elevation", she explained. "Still, they don't get the same prices because they are—Slovenians".

I was too tipsy to be sad about this. Instead, I took a nap and then, borrowing Maurizia's bike, went into town later on for dinner.

I decided to stay at Casa Mafalda for two nights. Actually, my body decided for me. After Maurizia's husband served breakfast the next morning, I slept some more and read in bed, looking out towards the historic town, two kilometres to the west. Cormons lies like a watchman (or a German shepherd) at the foot of the long hill of the Collio, resting in the middle of the whole area. For over two thousand years, there were power struggles between Gorizia, Cormons and Cividale. Attila the Hun destroyed Aquileia, the Langobards took over Cividale—but the wine farmers kept marrying within the villages and making good wine, as ever. This old Cormons was still here for me!

Discovering a town is like getting to know a person. Feeling a bit odd and different at first, one walks the streets again, reads some signs and gets to know the contours, the cafés and the plazas. I walked now in the daylight on a different path, one that lay close to the hills. There I discovered dozens of old villas and wine estates, some of them 500 years old or older. Stone walls, old vineyards, villas that had life and workers around them in 1450—1590—1650—were watching me pass by, frowning on my buoyant steps, wondering what I was doing in Cormons!

After getting to know the town a bit, I doubled back to a place that had attracted me at first sight. This was the only plaza in the town that had more space to breathe and a bit of old-city character. There was also a wine tasting house—the most creative and lively place I had seen so far. One could sit and snack on cheese, bread, and olives, read and at one's own speed, pick out wines from the entire Collio region—45 of them to choose from. There was time to taste and smell "the earth and the berries", as Marino would later say. Just one small glass at a time—that is how I did it! I read a book in between glasses and tasted, all toll, seven different wines. Yes!

That may have been the reason why I had such success with Barbara in the late afternoon! I stopped by a travel agency that specialized in tourism for that area. Barbara was cute, 25 and listened to my long story, astonishingly. I told her of my original plans, of the closed down agritourismo farms, of my decision not to follow the Isonzo River, but to go directly to Duino. Could she find a place in between—and in Duino, as well? "My feet will do the rest, Barbara", I joked with her.

She was unbelievably nice, efficient and charming—and she thought my project was not crazy, but very honourable! The most astonishing thing is that the people and the places she found for me provided an adventure I will never forget—and perhaps the best stories! You will have to read on or you will never find out!

THE OLD ROAD

Still round the corner there may wait
A new road or a secret gate;
And though I oft have passed them by,
A day will come at last when I
Shall take the hidden paths that run
West of the Moon, East of the Sun.

Frodo sings softly parts of the old "Walking-Song" to Sam, somewhat altered by Frodo himself.

JRR Tolkien, *Lord of the Rings*

"*Andiamo!* Let's go..." I said to myself and to my gnarly walking stick. With Barbara's reservations and handwritten addresses in my pocket, I hoisted the backpack onto my shoulders once again and prepared for the next leg of my journey. Barbara had called all over southeast Friuli to find the right spots to stay, as well as revealing a tricky way down to the ocean. This walking tour would only have been half as good without her negotiations with all sorts of Italian-cell-phone-holders throughout the countryside. At the moment, however, I did not realize it!

All I knew was that Maurizia sat in front of me and stroked the ears of that odd dog they all loved so much. Even the geriatric German shepherd liked that runt! Maurizia had the day off and her gentle old husband was sleeping off a hangover from the night before. He had gone out with the men who were seriously grieving the death of their old crony, one of the most respected men in the area over many decades. Then I looked at her.

"Maurizia", I said, putting my hand on my heart, "your husband is a good man. He has a good heart". She smiled and her eyes filled with tears. She knew what I meant and why I had said it.

"I know", she said softly, but resolutely. Then she looked over at the table under the oak tree where we drank wine together two days before. Her eyes took in the newly planted vineyards like someone who knew what hard work meant.

"Tom, take the old road", she said with conviction. "It's better". Then she pointed down the road towards the south: "Can you see where the road takes you through a small tunnel? That road will lead you under the railroad tracks and onto the highway to Gorizia. Don't take that road. Rather, turn left before you get to the railroad tracks and walk on that road instead. It's the old road to Gorizia that people have been taking since the Middle Ages. It will serve you better, at least for the first four miles", she said, accentuating the last line with an American accent she had learned 27 years ago in Ohio. "Fewer cars, believe me—and you might find some nice surprises along the way. The drivers will think you're crazy, anyways! Half the town is talking about you. Drop me a postcard and send it to Casa Mafalda…not to The Red Rooster"!

Grabbing my walking stick I said, "Ciao", and was off again, heading down the long drive to another dirt road. From the heights I was able to get a good parting view of Cormons, off to the right. Thinking of the old villas, a bit of history I had read days before drifted through my head.

The town has pre-Roman origins and acquired significant importance in the early Middle Ages, thanks to the presence of a "castrum", a small fortress on the nearby Mount Quarìn, which, in the year

610, survived the invasion of the Avars. I would have to visit this old castrum the next time, I thought. From 628 C.E. to 717 C.E., it became the main residence of the Patriarchs of Aquileia. Subsequently, it was given as a gift by Otto II to the Patriarch Rodoaldo, and then became the object of a dispute between the patriarchs and the Counts of Gorizia, who were to become its governors. Now I was heading towards that very Gorizia, the larger town that overshadowed this little wine hamlet.

I really didn't think that "half the town" was talking about me, but it made a good story for Maurizia. (Maybe just a quarter of the town.) The fields along the "old road" were beautiful as I set off again. I was once again so intoxicated by nature that it did not bother me that the train tracks were so near, or that it had started to rain on my head. The rain came and went over the next hour, but did not really get anything wet. "At least the sun is being merciful today", I said to my walking stick.

I was trying to find descriptions in my limited vocabulary of the type of beauty around me. The fields and roads were not immaculate and they were not showing off their forms and colours in a way that makes someone "ooh and awe". It was a type of simplicity mixed with a sort of luxury. It was the ever-changing hill contours that were seldom the same! In Austria I often have the feeling that many of the magnificent hills and mountains look pretty much the same. Here the hills and fields were constantly surprising me!

I walked around the town of Russiz, whose wine I had tasted in that amazing wine tasting house in Cormons. Soon the famous town of Capriva del Friuli could be seen in the distance. I had heard of this town because it had a golf course, of all things. The course was laid out nicely in between an old wine estate, some tourist flats and the rolling hills on the south side of the Collio. This was part of the luxury. I would have loved to change my plans and stay there! I almost did. The town was calling to me like the Sirens on the Greek island did to Ulysses. Instead, I played it tough, kept out of the sand traps and tramped on. I decided that I would stop for a beer at Mossa, the last village before Gorizia.

The most difficult part of the trip that day, however, began in Mossa. First of all, I had to walk on a street with no earth for my walking stick to grab hold of. Secondly, and most important, I missed the cosy atmosphere of most Italian towns. I checked out the area near the church: No café. I checked out various places, but nowhere was there a place to drink a beer! I had to look at my own prejudice—Slovenian culture, which had influenced this area over hundreds of years, was just different. It seemed to me a bit more sober and lacking colourful culture. At least there was fresh drinking water here, which I drew from an old well, filling my bottle. I sat in the shade under an old plane tree with its broad, light green leaves, thinking perhaps that all the good pubs and cafés were closed down now that the main tourist season had ended.

As I neared Gorizia and crossed the bridge over the Isonzo River, I was definitely in a bigger city! It was fun to march through the streets past all the cool kids hanging around as I now clacked my walking stick on pavement instead of the earth. There, among the bars in the streets of Gorizia, I found the right place for a beer.

Barbara had convinced me that the geography from Gorizia down to the village where my next bed and breakfast was located would be very difficult to reach on foot. The only road plunged into the forest of the Karst, that stony plateau I had heard so much about.

"You couldn't have seen that on the map you have", she had informed me politely, in her cute voice, "but I know that it is not a good place to walk. Trust me". So that is why I once again gave up my goal to walk instead of ride, taking a bus seven kilometres down to Iamiano. I trusted Barbara.

It took me an hour, however, to find the train station where I would catch the bus. I soon discovered I was on the wrong side of town. Sitting next to my backpack after the long detour, I propped my walking stick up on an old wall near the train station and waited for my bus. I thought of the fact that Gorizia had been divided—somewhat like East and West Berlin—up until 2007. That recently! The Yugoslavian Partisans occupied Gorizia for two months at the end of World War II. The Allies ran the administration until Italy took over Gorizia in 1947. Gorizia had always been a mixed-language city. For hundreds of years, the language representation was 70% Italian, 20% Slovenian and 10 % German—so this was nothing new.

In 1948, however, the authorities of the Socialist Republic of Slovenia (with president Tito's special support) started building a new town called *Nova Gorica* (New Gorizia) on their side of the border, where most of the Slovenian speaking people in the town lived. Although the situation in Gorizia was often compared with that of Berlin in the Cold War, I was informed that Italy and Yugoslavia had worked on keeping good relations regarding Gorizia, including promoting cultural and sporting events that favoured the spirit of harmonious coexistence. This remained in place after Yugoslavia broke up in 1991. With the breakup of Yugoslavia, the frontier remained as the division between Italy and Slovenia until the implementation of the Schengen Agreement by Slovenia on the 21st of December, 2007.

The bus finally arrived and the driver was a big dude. He told me to stash my backpack and walking stick in the passenger section of the bus. "Get in. You are the only passenger"!

"Why's that"? I asked, really curious, as I sat down across from him in this giant bus without passengers. It was almost like being in some Alfred Hitchcock film; I was waiting for something out of the ordinary to happen.

"It's like this", he said as he drove out of the city: "At this time of the day everybody is taking a siesta! The bus is full in the morning and in the late afternoon". Then I saw what Barbara had meant: The only road down to Monfalcone from here fed into a thick forest and with no place to walk on the side.

"Is there another way through the Karst to get down to Duino? I asked.

A WALK TO THE CROSSROADS / 69

"Well, yes, but it winds through the forest villages like a snake. You would need about nine hours by foot".

Next trip, I thought.

When we reached Iamiano, I jumped off the bus and let the big guy throw me the walking stick. As the bus took off down the road, the first thing I saw was a war memorial. The village was set back a bit, and on the street you felt as if there were no houses about, only old forest and rocks. Again, the war memorial told about a battle that had been fought here on this narrow road during the First World War. Even in this narrow village, a new memorial recently had been constructed to honour the dead and work through the events of the past. I just stood there awhile, leaning on my walking stick.

What transpired then was uncanny. I started to think about looking for my lodging when all of a sudden it started looking for me, as so often happened. I found an old farmhouse two houses down the road, even though I had not yet started looking for the house numbers. As I walked around to its inner courtyard, wondering if anyone was around, I was fascinated by the colour of the blue shutters on the old windows. It was like an old farmhouse out of the 16th century that had just had its shutters painted with the slight glacial turquoise colour of the Soča River in Slovenia.

Suddenly a woman spoke to me from behind an old apple tree. "*Attenzione,* are you the American looking for a room"?

I said: "*Si, Signora*".

She laughed and said, "Come on over to the garden", as she opened the door for me. She spoke English poorly, but had mastered a few phrases, butchering them thoroughly. "Here, this man speaks German", she said. "He can translate". The old man, about 80, was obviously the farmer who lived there, the rest of his family already gone or dead. He looked pretty fit. He also let me know that he had no gumption to translate, but would rather talk about his farm in the old days.

"This path going up the hill over to the next valley used to be the old road from the Isonzo River over to our village", he recounted in an old German accent. The signora interrupted (as she was apt to do for the next two days) and said: "I'll show you to your room".

"Is the room in this old farmhouse"? I inquired.

"*No. Attenzione:* It's up on the older road", she said pedantically. "I was just down here visiting my neighbour".

Her modern house up the old road looked nice, but it did not have any soul like the old farmhouse did. She showed me to my room in a dark cellar, filled with really tacky paintings. It was musty and the bathroom had mildew. A steep step led downwards to my room and the entire place was predestined to be a disaster. I thought: *The World War I tanks should move in again and blow this up.* I would have preferred her neighbour's old farmhouse with its blue shutters, I mused, as I set my backpack and walking stick down in the room. The old man surely needed someone to talk to.

The old road leading up the hill and away from the farmhouse, however, held surprises—as always. It was there that I met Francesco.

Francesco

Every joy is beyond all others.
The fruit we are eating is always
the best fruit of all.

C.S. Lewis, Perelandra

I did not like Francesco at all at our first encounter. Wrapped in a towel after his shower and slinging his *macho-Italian-man* image through the hallway, he seemed in need of recognition for some reason. The signora had summoned the two of us to have a small, dark-hallway conference, seeing as I had asked if anyone was driving into town to grab a bit to eat that evening. Once again, I was stuck way out in the boonies, away from any restaurants.

I watched and listened for over five minutes as they heatedly discussed (in a heavy dialect that was hard to understand) whether and how this might happen. I tried to read their body language, wondering if she was asking him for a favour, or why, for heaven's sake, they were disputing so long. Francesco extrapolated with exasperation, like many Italians do when all they are talking about is how to cook noodles! It sounded like he wanted to attack Saddam Hussein or an uncle who had robbed him of 200,000 euros.

After putting up with this for what seemed to me a decade, he agreed to drive to town and get a pizza with me. I was glad that he felt obliged to offer me a ride.

"*Alle otto*"! he said.

"Et Oh'Klockeh"! the signora over-lipped it—and, in case I had shut off my hearing aid—she yelled again: "Et Oh'Klockeh! Okay"?

"Eight o'clock is fine", I assured her.

I had no problem with seven, eight, or nine! We were stranded in a B&B in a forest area between Gorizia and Monfalcone and I was thankful for any way to get some food. She had offered a lower rate than most, the price being only 26 euros a night and at that moment, stuck in the cellar with Francesco, the mildew and the signora, I suddenly knew why the price was so low! I was going to ask the signora, who was well over 60 (trying to look 25 again) if she had painted or sketched some of the hundreds of obnoxiously tacky paintings that hung in the dank halls of her B&B. But I thought better of it, not knowing whether I would offend or flatter her!

Escaping the cellar as quickly as possible, I sat on the veranda waiting for "Et Oh'klockeh" when Francesco would whisk me away to some place where I could get a good meal. After walking those ten kilometres to Gorizia —with breakfast memories at Maurizia's dating back to 9 a.m.—I was more than ready. Smoking a pipe seemed like a good way to save the early evening from becoming a minor disaster, so I lit one up! Suddenly, the veranda came alive as the signora broadcast music for her B&B guests. She had tuned her radio to an Italian-pop station, which seethed through the loud speakers into our veins, barely soothing our basement blues.

While working on my pipe, I tried to read a section of Henri Nouwen's meditations on Rembrandt's painting, *The Return of the Prodigal Son,* which is hanging in the Hermitage. I suddenly noticed that dirt from a broken flowerpot—a lot!—was sifting into the back of my sandals! I thought: *Well, the signora probably has a heavy load and just doesn't get around to cleaning everything.* Then I noticed the cobwebs under the table that, just between us, looked like they had somehow missed the spring-cleaning of 1968! The magazines and plants were nice, and the house looked like a modern mainstream museum with its faux etchings and statues. I suddenly placed my hopes on Francesco—the signora being the first person I have had to bear with patience this whole week—that he might quickly appear and rescue me from this veranda.

When Francesco arrived I could not see him because he was standing in the garden below. The signora signalled to me to hurry up and come.

"*Attenzione!* You cum"! As I packed up my pipe and small knapsack she repeated: "You cum"!

"*Si, si, Signora. Piano*"! I said, trying to figure out why she had a need to command my life after only three hours.

Francesco and I headed out the gate, passing the old farmhouse where I had stopped when I arrived, and climbed into his Opel. We both knew from the start that it would be an Anglo/Ital-linguistic-adventure. His English was almost non-existent, or so it seemed, and my Italian was lacking some finesse, although I liked to think it was better.

"My French is worse", I told him.

How would we communicate, I mused, as the forest flew by in the dusty dusk of south Friuli.

We pulled into a pizzeria along the coast and looked for a table. I soon noticed that Francesco was a practical, meat-and-potatoes man. Feeling our differences, I wondered what we would talk about with our mega-linguistic lack? Maybe we would not talk at all! After he ordered his meal and I my special arugula, mozzarella, olive and garlic pizza, we drank our beers and wondered about bilingual possibilities. Two men trying to be cool.

Then it happened.

As is often the case, when I tell someone that I am a Lutheran pastor and an American, to boot, he wanted to move into political-theological-philosophical issues. Appearing as if we were playing poker with high stakes, he crouched slowly, like a jaguar, moving in for the kill:

"Okay. George Bush. *Buono oppure non buono*"? (Good or bad?)

I said with conviction: *"Non buono"*! I was okay! The evening was saved and I had not sold my soul to do it.

The jaguar crouched again: "Eh, Israel? *Bouno oppure non buono*"?

I was trapped, but blundered around in the best Italian I could dig up and said: *"Alcune persone sono in gamba, alcune persone di meno, alcuni partiti sono buoni altri invece sono troppo radicali"*. (Some people are OK, others not; some political parties are good, others are too radical.) He was semi-satisfied. We went through several of these hunting games until Francesco's pasta arrived. After a while, Francesco's meat and potatoes arrived, as well.

I was served nothing. We practiced diplomacy.

When my pizza arrived, it did not look like the one I had ordered. Fried egg in the middle, hot dog pieces and imitation olives was how I described it. Oh, no! Did I not understand the Italian description in the menu? I tell you, I was really hungry!

At the table behind us, a man spoke to me in English and in German: "Did something get mixed up"?

"Maybe, I said", turning around to face him.

My neighbour then said: "That looks like the pizza I ordered".

I figured that it was too late to send it back, seeing as I had already taken a bite, so I cut a piece off and handed it over on a napkin to the neighbour. He laughed and took it, saying: "Yes, this was my pizza"!

A few seconds later my pizza finally arrived, at his table! We both realized what had happened as I saw the fresh tomatoes, big olives and arugula. I said right out: "Well, let's just switch"!

He nodded, so I carried his pizza over (with one-and-a-half missing pieces) and took mine with loving care back to our table. We laughed, immensely satisfied.

Big, bulky Francesco had been watching all this with his mouth open, shaking his head back and forth. Suddenly he laughed with an inner and freeing implosion. *I think I am hallucinating—in Italy this would never take place in a restaurant*—was the best I could make out from his expressions and words.

It was a quiet revolution. In that simple restaurant the ice was broken, as can happen on any day, anywhere in the world. Francesco then started chuckling from the inside out at the pure audacity of the "Grande Pizza Exchango". Some kind of cultural and heart transformation had taken place. I was very happy. My neighbour was happy. Francesco was bewildered, but was, without acknowledging it, also happy. Something had happened—and this storyteller is not exaggerating!

"Ma", he uttered. I knew this expression was used in Italy. It means roughly: *But, oh man—this is wild and curious—and we're stuck between a rock and a hard place—it makes me think—and, I can't believe this*—all in one. "Ma"! he said again.

The pizza was *buona*! Francesco occasionally threw out statements that I didn't understand. My neighbour, trying to be polite, did his best to translate from the table behind me. Then, for a while, Francesco just stared at me, his head in his hand. *Silenzio*.

I presently said, "I eat slowly, right"? (He had finished his meal earlier.) To translate this I asked my neighbour again. "How does one say 'slowly'"?

"*Lento*".

Ah, of course, from music! What a dummy I am. "*Io mangio molto lento, vero*"? I offered, as I picked out the arugula out of my teeth, trying to be polite to this

Italian macho who, all of a sudden winked at me, showing his human and playful side.

"Let's go for a *Gelato* after you are finished: '*Ice Cream*'," he translated for me. "We'll drive to Monfalcone", he continued in Italian, "the place where I have been working on the big ships. It's a big industrial town but has a lot of culture, too—and I know the best *Gelato* place"!

Francesco chattered away as if I truly understood everything he was saying as we drove into the harbour city of Monfalcone. It was as if we were buddies now and he wanted to show me his community—his world. He somehow got across that he had worked there for eleven years and recently had worked on building and renovating cabins on the new cruise ship—The Queen Elisabeth—"300 meters long", he emphasized!

As we entered the famous ice cream parlour and ordered our cones, (he had insisted on paying!) he said, once again, "Ma"! It had become our joke.

I shot back a sarcastic, "Ma", making fun of the Italians who always said that, and he caught my sarcasm. At the same time we both knew that it was a humorous commentary on our communication barrier. It was as if "Ma" was all we had. We could connect!

"Ma"! He said after 10 seconds—to increase the dramatic effect. The ice was broken, floating like an iceberg across the harbour water.

"Ma"! I countered again.

Soon, Francesco began to reveal the story of his life. As we walked through the main plaza in Monfalcone taking in the immense buildings from the Habsburg Era and the beauty of the town, I contemplated that I was not prepared for the unexpected beauty and depth in him—this "macho"! One of his two sons was severely handicapped—physically and mentally. His wife cared for him, daily. The pain and love he felt for his son and the true appreciation he showed for his wife, moved and surprised me. I realized then that Francesco was someone who was able to show his vulnerability.

"I will drive home tomorrow to be with them", he said. "Three weeks of building ship berths here has not been easy—knowing that my wife is caring for my son almost completely on her own—but it is work that I must do, honest work. Now it's time to go home. Tomorrow morning. *Domani*". Francesco, void of upper middle class smiles and intellectual games, spoke down-to-earth truth. "*Andiamo?* Let's head back to the B&B", he said.

"Okay", I answered. I didn't even want to joke about the signora. Who knew whether she was a wild card, or an oddball relative who also needed his care.

As we drove back he took an alternative route, winding along unfamiliar roads near Monfalcone. He started to talk rapidly, forgetting that I only caught titbits of what he was saying. He began to throw out dozens of *"Perchè"?* (why?) questions, with earnest and playful questions mixed together!

"*Perchè?* Why do men and women always end up with so many unresolved issues? *Perchè?* Why does God allow war? *Perchè?* Why didn't God make the flood come to Sudan, where they need water, instead of to Pakistan"? Soon I knew that Francesco was serious. *"Perchè?* Why does God allow bad things to happen to innocent people—why does he allow children to get cancer or be handicapped"?

I felt solemnly and heartfully put to the test. I grasped enough to understand the questions, the questions that plague us all! What should I answer? He pressed through the night as we neared the signora's place—through the forest of the Karst—with its stone foundation. Honestly, I was not sure that I could give answers in any form—especially in broken Italian—that would do any good at all!

Finally, though, I sputtered out a kind of an answer. While we left the lights of Monfalcone behind, I tried in my best Italian: *"I piccoli bambini sono molto importanti e l'amore è la base di tutto. È fondamentale quanto i sassi nel carsto".* (Small children and small people in society remain important in God's eyes and love is the foundation of everything, just like the rocks of the Karst.)

Francesco pressed again with further *"Perchè"* questions. I answered the same way, thinking he had not heard me. Then he quietly said: *"Si, capisco".* Had he understood? Was my answer even a start at being enough? All of a sudden he said in perfect English: "I have a dream"!

What was coming now? I asked myself. It was 1 a.m. in the forest, in the Friuli fog. Why had he faked not knowing English the whole time? Did he want to talk about Martin Luther King now?

Francesco stopped the car and turned off the engine. I had no idea where we were because he had taken a different route. I quickly turned around to see if we were near the B&B. He sat still, looking around at the streets.

Suddenly there arose in me an irrational fear. Maybe I couldn't trust him after all, I thought. I had no idea, really, who this guy was! Was he going to rob me, or worse? Something weird? Did I completely misread his heart as he opened up to me and as we joked about "Ma"?

"I have a dream," he said again. Another minute went by.

Then he smiled, winked at me and drove slowly around the corner slicing off some bushes along the way. He parked the car right smack in front of the farmhouse with the signora's house behind it!

"I had a dream..." He laughed, and then said in Italian, "that I would find a better parking spot for this old car! I just needed some time to think and look around. I need to leave at 6 a.m. and don't want to spend time looking for the car in the foggy morning! My family is waiting".

Oh mercy! I thought, lying on my bed that night. May I never stop learning to trust my intuition. That's why God gave it to you, Preston—

Ma!

Francesco snored so loudly that night in the adjacent room that the walls were shaking! Who cares, I thought to myself. I can sleep in Duino. Besides, that guy is my friend now! I'm part of his community.

Francesco was on his way home.

Timavo at the Crossroads

*I will show you hidden things
that you have not known.*

Isaiah 48:6, *Old Testament, New English Bible Translation*

The overworked and overambitious signora, trying to be creative with the atmosphere at the B&B, played Italian pop music again during our breakfast on the veranda. The music and the news blurbs (imitating American style) seemed like Mozart to my ears because it drowned out her scratchy voice. I had already been mesmerized by the radio in my basement room an hour earlier; the only air in the cellar flowed through a screen on the terrace floor and her nifty music speakers vibrated the cover screen. My only consolation was that I would soon be on my way again. My walking tour through Italian Friuli on the rim of the Adriatic would soon take on new contours!

I had a lot of energy and anticipation as I set off early that morning. Passing the farm along the "old road", I hoped to see the old German-speaking farmer again. I sought some melody to hum, thinking that I might lure him out of the farmyard with my song. I chuckled at myself, realizing that I was really trying to sing away the "signora blues"! I never saw the old man again, but I hoped he would keep telling stories about the history of the old road!

It wasn't far to Duino, only seven kilometres. It's odd, when I think back, that I had very few expectations about the town or of the area surrounding it. I had taken along a few computer pictures of the Rilke Path, which I had planned explore while I was in the area, but that was it, and that was good! I was truly surprised by what I encountered on my way to Duino. The landscape I had covered the night before with Francesco on our drive from Iamiano to the pizzeria was familiar, but looked different in daylight. On the road down to the coast, the forest was just as thick as ever. My walking stick gouged the fresh earth on the right as my hiking boots plodded along the street.

Suddenly (and very suddenly!) the forest ended, and on the right side to the southwest, a beautiful panorama opened up! The whole upper Adriatic, the harbour of Monfalcone and the coastline towards Grado appeared before my eyes. It was great! I did not know how elevated the road from Gorizia was above the city—it was somewhat of a revelation. I also saw the places southwest of Monfalcone that my son Michael and I had scoped out a month earlier, thinking then that the harbour was not very attractive. I looked out into the distance where, over centuries, the Isonzo River had created the long delta that curved out into the water. I checked the map briefly to discover that this gulf area was not simply the north Adriatic, but was called "Golfo di Parzano", to be exact.

The fact that Monfalcone was an industrial and shipbuilding city, with its cranes, ships and smokestacks, could not hinder the beauty of the town seen from above. Once again, I leaned on my walking stick as I looked out towards the harbour and thought about a lot of things—for instance, how perspectives change from time to time. I thought of my talks with Francesco on those streets the night before. I thought about the difference of moving back into my walking mode, entering into a different perspective! I heard the river Isonzo speaking to me from a distance, like the Judrio and the Natisone Rivers had a few days before, saying: "Here I am, Tom—but your path does not lie with me this time—another river awaits your coming"!

I looked around again in the other direction and took in the stony personality of this new area. I was standing on the threshold of the Karst! It starts here and spreads out north of Trieste, the main part of its rocky terrain running through southern Slovenia. This is that historical, geographical area I had heard about!

A few vineyards were scattered along the southern Italian hills, but the land to the north was forest and farmland with it's varied, stony undergirding pocketed with thousands of caves, springs and potholes. Karst waters supply more than half of the population in the area with drinking water, much of it brought to the surface from deep underground. The word for the *Karst* region in Slovenia is known as *Kras*. The deep stony character of the Karst, however, showed itself best along the white rocky coast of Italy, where I was headed.

I managed to shake myself from marvelling, donned my backpack and took to the road again. Now I was heading east, in the direction of Trieste. As I walked again on the "old road", (this time the old road wound from Rome over ancient Aquileia to Istria and the coast on the eastern side of the Adriatic), I was amazed at how the rocky coast and hills showed immense patience with the old railroad line and the new Autostrada. It was quite impressive, really, how the Autostrada had been cut into the rocks of the coastal edge of the Karst, creating a "give and take" with the old railroad line.

On the east side of Monfalcone was a ravine where the Karst plateau started. There, directly over the ravine, was an impressive railroad bridge that reminded me of the work of Mussolini, possibly with a little help from Hitler. They were both anxious to control the Balkan region, the area that became Yugoslavia after the war. (The Slavs were just as anxious not to be in either of their claws!) I had a geographic crossroads experience every few meters, as I poked my walking stick into stone now, instead of earth. Something else was waiting for me around the next curve!

I kept walking and watching the Autostrada and the rocky terrain. This Italian freeway eventually crossed paths with me and plunged under the old road, then wound along the hills behind Duino. Then, with only three kilometres left until I reached the town, I came to another crossroads. An older and smaller road plunged down from the middle of the Karst to the north and joined the road to Duino.

On a cliff overlooking this crossroads was a village named San Giovanni al Timavo, with its old church and a few houses, next to which stood a large war memorial and graveyard. Across the street from the church on the southern side was a stone outcropping upon which stood two wolves carved out of stone. On the lower part of the outcropping was another war memorial with all sorts of things written upon it in Italian, Slovenian and Latin. I was curious, but was distracted by my search for shade as it was already nearing noon and the sun was practicing its old tricks.

I spontaneously turned off the road in the direction of the coast, having spotted a shady area under a grove of huge towering trees. The road had levelled out a bit and I felt like I was closer to the sea, but I could not tell where the coast of the Adriatic started, because the trees were hiding the view. My sense was that the coast was about one kilometre away.

I had seen some water from the road and wondered where the source was. Was there water coming from the ravine and flowing under the railroad bridge—or was this an inland harbour? I wandered around a bit. No, I thought, the colour of the water was too blue-greenish, like the upper Isonzo River, or the emerald Soča where I swam with my son near Caporetto, Slovenia.

Stepping further into the shady area under the giant trees, I noticed an old hydroelectric plant of some sort, looking like it too had been built before the last war. The stones and architecture were of that period. Walking further along the path, I saw a floodgate in front of me surrounded by more trees and heard the strong current of water rushing through it. What was this? Where was the water coming from, I wondered, half consciously, half intuitively. A few more steps revealed, of all things, a very old chapel surrounded by old oak and plane trees.

At that moment, an Italian tour guide who had good command of the English language walked towards me across a bridge over the rushing water. He was about to translate some signs posted in Italian for his English visitors, and I hoped that he could solve the riddle for me. "What is this"? I asked, unabashed.

He replied: "You're right to ask, this is something special. It is the spot where the Timavo flows out of the cliffs! For thirty-five kilometres this somewhat unknown river disappears in Slovenia. No one knows where she flows. She runs underground somewhere deep in the Karst and then reappears—here—cascading out of those small cliffs over there! The Timavo then joins two smaller streams that flow out of nearby cliffs, and together they rush to the sea"!

As I looked around me, then back to the cliff, my jaw dropped. Ah, yes! This was the river my friend spoke of one day at the school where we teach together. Thinking he had been talking about the Isonzo River, I had checked the maps again and again, trying to figure out where this "disappearing act" took place. I thought that he had perhaps exaggerated, but he had been so adamant that it seemed worth checking out. Now, here it was!

"Yes", the Italian man went on, "in ancient times the people thought that this was a very magical, mysterious and sacred place"! (Actually, the place reminded me of an ancient Druid forest.) He went on to explain: "On the altar of that gothic chapel over there, you can see unique archaeological diggings and mosaics from an early church in the third century, around the time of the height of Aquileia's power. Some of it is of Roman origin, and parts of the diggings have ties to the legend of Hercules"! Then he turned to his guests and walked on.

I was truly fascinated, and still had many questions about historical and scientific information about the Timavo River. That could come later. First, I wanted to check this place out! I stood still, leaning on my staff for a few minutes, just watching the source of the Timavo. Then I scooped up some water from the swift moving current that slowed as it formed a deep pool. I wanted see how cold it was, but did not drink from it.

Walking across the yard, I found the entry of the chapel on the backside, away from the river. As I stepped through the door, I noticed that the chapel itself was more beautiful from the outside. I was impressed by the fact that the whole area had somehow remained simple and undisturbed. Maybe visitors over the centuries had felt the stillness alongside the surging waters. Maybe the trees had been planted hundreds of years ago for that purpose.

Once outside again, I walked along an old wall leading away from the pool and the church. It was like walking through the overgrown remains of a special rampart and garden of The Middle Ages. There I saw, off to the left, the spot where a second part of the Timavo merged with the first stream. It rushed out from under thick brush and then through the old hydroelectric dam and floodgate.

A sign was posted alongside the floodgate: *Absolutely no fishing, scuba diving or swimming!* I pondered why this was so. It looked so refreshing! A few days later I found out the reason. Everybody had some story to tell about the Timavo. One student I met on the rocks overlooking the bay in Duino said that her father, a history professor, found out that there had been mines laid in the Timavo during the Second World War. Someone had apparently wanted to hinder soldiers from sneaking into the harbour further downstream. The mines were still active and potentially could explode! They were like the old bombs that the Americans dropped on Salzburg at the end of the war that still exploded occasionally when dug up! This was the main reason for the *No Swimming* sign.

In spite of hoards of stinging mosquitoes, I decided to sketch the cliff and pool where the Timavo welled up out of nowhere. An old stone wall had been built on top of the cliff. Above that was a small hill, and above that, the main road! *So exposed and unprotected on that side*, I thought. The pool itself was only seven by ten meters. It was in its natural state until it artificially narrowed through the floodgates. After a few meters, it expanded again along the groves of giant trees. I checked my detailed map and found the small letters: "*Fonte del Timavo*". On the map one could see the branches flowing into a small ocean village and harbour—Villagio del Pescatore—and then into the Adriatic Sea.

Scouring information stemming from old Roman writings, I found interesting historical notes about the nine sources of the Timavo and the terrible noise the vast waters made when the water rushed out the cliffs. Scientists have found, only recently, that there are several sources for the Timavo—one of them the Reka River in Slovenia—but the experts are not unanimous in their opinion! It still remains a bit of a mystery.

After awhile, the mosquitoes were eating me up, so I decided to move on, having resolved to come back soon! Since I had made a sketch of the waters, cliff, stone wall, hill and the street above them, the thought occurred to me that right above the Timavo was another crossroads. In Roman times this old road was called "Via Germana" (the German Road), which linked Aquilea to Trieste. Italy, Slovenia, Austria and the Balkans meet here—and the Timavo flows underneath it all!

Up on the road to Duino again, I looked to the right at the two wolves on the cliff above. I climbed up a bit on the outcropping across from the church and tried to see the plaques on the memorial above me. As far as I could understand from the inscriptions in Italian, it was a war memorial for both wars. One plaque said something profound in Latin: *"The Timavo teaches us and refreshes us. Let us learn from it"!*

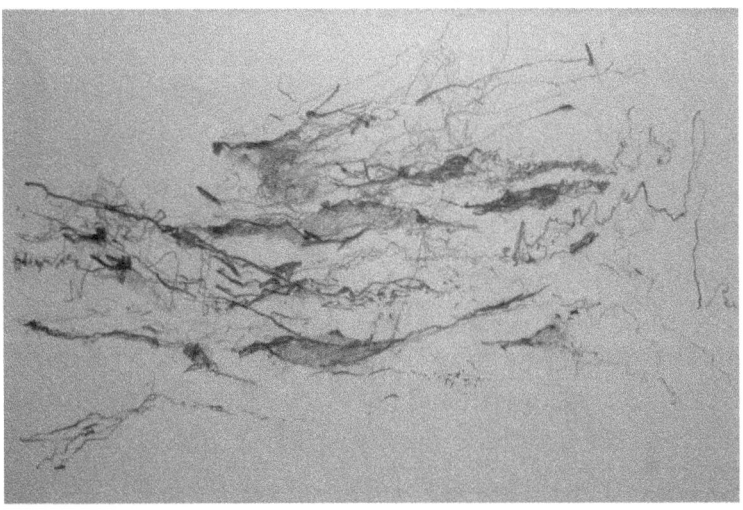

The two stone wolves stood, tense and awake, on the peak. I tapped around with my walking stick like a blind man, meditating on all of this. Although I found out that the wolves were meant to be a warning to those coming out of the north, the reoccurring thought emerged:

> *Why am I again (twice daily!) confronted with the historical consequences of both world wars? What kind of suffering went on at these crossroads? Up the valley in Caporetto? Along the Isonzo? Thousands upon thousands of soldiers—Italian, Slovenian, German, Serb, Austrian, Croatians—had been killed brutally, seemingly meaninglessly—caught in the crossroads of national scheming and interest—fighting out old animosities! The Timavo hides its head as if embarrassed, and then reappears. It closes its eyes for thirty-five kilometres and then, humbly, unobtrusively and swiftly flows into the sea, refreshing, renewing and teaching.*

My faithful walking stick and I were on our way again. I walked the last three kilometres to Duino at the hottest time of the day, between 2 and 3 p.m., when many were taking a siesta. I was curious about Duino. The ocean—when would I see it? *The sea around Monfalcone didn't really count,* I said to myself. My goal had been to walk to the sea and then dive in! Just like my kids (and just like I did as a kid), I tended to wait for the first honest view of the sea before I said *"Hurrah"!* After awhile I walked past the sloping road leading to Villagio Pescatore, its harbour created by the Timavo as it meets the sea. I had planned to explore it a bit, but kept pressing on.

When I finally arrived in Duino, I was impressed by its smallness. I was glad that it was not a big tourist village, but still had to ask around a bit to find my lodging. The number "61-D" did not seem to fit into any logical pattern I could find, as I compared it with the numbers on the street. My impression was that it was a small flat a few hundred meters up from a small harbour.

Finally, upon asking for some help, one woman smiled and said: *"Ah, si, si!* Just keep walking down the road, then around a few curves, until you can't walk anymore without falling into the sea! Then you'll see it".

As if everyone wanted to surprise me (not the least, Barbara, the cute travel agent in Cormons) I finally arrived at a quaint restaurant on the harbour. The name on the handwritten note matched the name of the Restaurant: "Al Cavalluccio". That was it! The woman I had asked was right: Two or three steps further and I would land in the water! With backpack, gnarly walking stick and sunglasses, I walked to the patio with tables. Some people were drinking wine, some eating lunch. I promptly asked the first waiter I met: *"Scusi!* Is there some mistake? I have a room reservation here and this is a restaurant"!

"No, Si! Un momento! I'll get Marino, the boss".

As I waited for the boss I thought, OK, there will probably be some flat back up the road that belongs to the owner.

Then he came out, checking his book. "What was your name"? he asked, as the man next to us motioned for more wine.

"Preston"! I said.

"Ah! Here it is. Someone almost scribbled over it. Your room is right up there", he said, pointing to the balcony above. I could almost have touched it with my walking stick. "Can you see it? It overlooks the harbour! Best room in Duino! When you open the shutters in the morning you can almost jump into the water! *Benissimo!* But the room will not be ready for another two hours. Sit down and relax; I'll bring you some wine"!

"Ma"! Once again—blessed out of my socks! Could things get any better? It was a cheaper room because, as I found out, I had to wriggle through the kitchen and around a maze of waiters to get up a somewhat greasy stairway. But it was all worth it, one hundred per cent! The view, the harbour, feeling the sea breeze—it was more than great! *Fantastico!*

I sat there, drank some cold wine and ate an *Insalata Caprese*, taking it all in. My backpack and walking stick leaned up against the terrace near the table, as if I had been at home there for weeks! I hadn't even put my feet in the water yet. That could wait until my room was ready, I reasoned, as I drank the last drop of my Sauvignon Blanc.

I was so awed by the situation that I had forgotten to say *"Hurray"!* when I viewed the sea, so I raised my glass to the waiter, José, and said: "Hurray! *Benissimo*"! Then he served me pasta and a glass of Friulano, chilled perfectly! As he served it he exclaimed: "È fantastico!—Nicht wahr"? mixing Italian and German. He sounded as if he wanted to convey something to the effect of *"today the pasta was better than anyone has tasted it for over 20 years"!* After three days of dining at Al Cavalluccio, I noticed that he said this about almost every dish and to almost every person, and I was always convinced! The others were convinced, as well!

I moved into my room, placing my walking stick carefully behind the door. Then I went out to the harbour wall and noticed that there was only one place to dive into the water. I dove in and swam and swam. I swam for one hour along the white cliffs of Duino as if I were a dolphin! Just taking in the green and yellow flowers growing out of the white cliffs that jutted out of the bay was marvellous! Lying on my back in the water and looking up at the old ruins of the 12th century Duino Castle, was already enough vacation for me! I was learning from the Timavo and I just let it flow! The water was unexpectedly clear and cold compared to the shallow and warmer waters of Grado where I swam with my son a month earlier. I later learned that my beloved Timavo, as it flowed out from the cove two kilometres away, mixed its cool fresh water with the warmer salt water of the sea. Swimming in Duino, the upper two meters were cold. As I dove down the water was warmer! The Timavo was refreshing me already!

It dawned on me during the next few days that the Timavo was in so many ways a "crossroads prophet", and not only geographically or historically. For me, it formed the crossroads between the end of the walking tour through the hillsides of Friuli, and the beginning of an important time of inner reflection and creativity in this special harbour village.

AL CAVALLUCCIO

*Anyone who thinks
that anything in life
is completely controllable
has become a stranger
to the cultures of the world.*

Gernot Candolini, Labyrinths: Walking Toward the Center

A better spot could not have been found for this stage of my journey. After six days of walking through the vineyards and villages of southeastern Friuli, my goal had been reached! I had walked to the sea and now was in the upper room of a cosy restaurant nestled into the edge of the small Duino Harbour. The situation looked like this: If I had the gumption to jump out my window after my shower, I would land naked on the table of the Austrians below, the whole crowd bellowing in snobbish Viennese dialect. A funny picture at that! If, on the other hand, I climbed out the window, scaled the side ridge and reached the stairs to the beach, I literally could dive into the ocean, which lapped the shore only ten meters in front of me!

At the far edge of the stone harbour wall was a special place from which one could dive into the Adriatic Sea and swim along the white cliffs that lined the coast. The water was immensely refreshing there! A mixture of salt and sweet waters, it was cooled by the flow of the Timavo River from the adjacent cove. The water was deep enough to dive from the cliffs above, but placid enough to swim for hours along the cliffs of Duino without saltwater waves tossing water in one's mouth!

My dream came true, without even knowing I had been dreaming or longing for it! From that point on I just read and wrote and did what came. I would swim, then sit in the restaurant below my room and drink wine, eat a snack, then take a nap—or write.

A humorous aspect of my stay at Al Cavalluccio involved the journey to the rooms upstairs. To reach my room I had to pass by the bar, squeeze through the narrow hallway to the kitchen, open a greasy door and edge my way upstairs—passing the wine buckets, napkin supply area and old pictures of Duino Castle from 1890. Each time I slithered past them on the way to my room, I met part of the staff. It was a bonding experience!

The first time going up the staircase I still had my hiking boots on, as well as my backpack and walking stick. The backpack nearly knocked over the plates of pasta José was carrying. I reminisced about the early seventies when American students touring Europe (me included) wore those Dachstein hiking boots (the ones with the red shoelaces) even in the summertime. They were the same boots that Steven Stills wore on the album cover of *Crosby Stills and Nash* in 1971. The boots always got in the way, humorously symbolizing obnoxious Americans pretending to be "back to nature freaks", when they were really just suburban kids traipsing around the small towns in Europe in their high-topped alpine hiking boots.

The second time I went down the stairs, I met Laura going by with the breadsticks and we brushed "tits and ass", as it were. The staff was all used to it and winked at me constantly. I thought it was hilarious!

"Hey, Tom. "*Come va?* Do you need a table to write on or to eat on tonight—or both"? was the question I would get from the staff, as I squeezed by the fish tank aquarium crawling with live lobsters. Miroslav would ask me which wine I wanted as he rushed by me to deliver his prawns with *aglio olio* to the Italian couple at the first table: "Slovenian or Italian wine"? In the morning when I took a swim, Ana whisked me through the back door while she washed the floors.

After two days in Duino I felt at home, as if I had lived there for a month or two already. This was not because the restaurant employees were practicing *treat the tourist like a king so that he will come again,* but rather it had to do with how they all worked together. It is seldom that one meets a group of servers, cooks and helpers who work so well as a team. They welcomed their guests in a way that revealed the secret behind their hosting qualities. This became so obvious that I soon began to praise them and comment on their teamwork.

As I first got to know Marino, the owner and "big boss", and then developed a friendship with him, it became clear that his style and communication were some of the reasons for the good teamwork, but only in part. Marino was a gentle man who, at 63 years old, had gone through a lot already and had developed and nurtured this now well-loved restaurant for over twenty years. I talked to guests who had been coming there year after year. Many of them drove down from southern Austria just to eat at Al Cavalluccio, take a swim and then drove home the same evening! I was convinced that many of them returned simply because they connected with the family atmosphere and convivial spirit.

Next door to Al Cavalluccio was the restaurant and bar that liked to think of itself as "the noble place" in Duino. I tried to eat there once and they kindly threw me out because I did not have a reservation. The real reason, I thought, was that I did not fit their image. Imagine that? At my age! It reminded me of the high school principal (our "pal") in 1965, who actually measured the guys' hair with a ruler! We risked being thrown out of school for enjoying our long hair, no joke! In addition, in front of the place next door was the only sandy beach—it measured a luxurious five-by-two meters. Unfortunately, the wait staff, restaurant and beach didn't have much soul. Most people liked hanging out at Al Cavalluccio.

This "snob palace", as I liked to call it, was named *"La Dama Bianca"*. The name came from the feminine shape of the rock formation in the middle part of the cliffs below the old ruins of the medieval castle. It looked like a lovely woman's figure wrapped in a white flowing cloak. This name also fit the waiters of the "snob palace", who all wore white and rarely smiled. At Al Cavalluccio there was no need to work on an image! They were the image! They were real. They smiled because they wanted to smile! The food was better, too.

Why am I writing about all of this? *This was supposed to be a story about the walking tour,* someone might say. *It belongs to the second half*—I would answer—*to the reflection period*. The people who worked at Al Cavalluccio helped me to feel at home, to do it right, whatever happened! That is why this incredible team deserves a chapter.

José has already been introduced. His pasta almost landed in the lobster aquarium a few times as he balanced the plates of food along the narrow passageway, but he always recovered with a good joke and tussled my hair a bit. José was the one who put wine on the table soon after I arrived and said, *"Fantastico"!* He was the hearty greeter who made everyone feel alive and welcome, even if they didn't want to be alive or welcomed! You could tell by his eyes that he had thousands of stories to tell, but his language skills in German and English were limited. His Italian was much better, but his mother tongue was Spanish!

I found out the real stories about the staff by talking to Marino, who spoke English very well. Marino commented on "Gustaf", as he had renamed José, "Yeah, he comes from Argentina, Tom. He has been my right hand man for over 20 years now". Marino added, "Before I came here he had already worked at Duino Castle during the seventies and eighties. He's the best"!

I had noticed a book that José had written when I visited the Duino Castle. He worked there for many years as headwaiter and had entertained dignitaries from all over the world. The book was filled with anecdotes about his encounters.

I must have looked, at that moment, like Arwen when she asked Aragorn how old he was in the extended film version of *Lord of the Rings*. "Wow! He must be ancient"! I said. "He doesn't look a day over 40"!

"Ha! He's 63; like me", Marino whispered. "But don't tell anyone. He wants the women to think he is 39"!

I sipped some Friulano with Marino (he just drank an espresso) and prompted him to tell me more.

"Gustaf has a son in Argentina", he said. "His marriage didn't work out, but he goes back to visit his son when he can".

"Huh? When did he have time to get married if he was always here"? I asked.

"He works hard here in Italy for seven months and then goes back to Argentina between November and March. Half of our team does something similar. They have other jobs in between or can afford to relax in the winter months. It's a little like the vintners in the rest of Friuli. They do not have too much to do after harvesting the grapes and bottling their wine, but for seven months they work their tails off! In the winter they reflect a lot—like you—here in Duino"!

"Okay. So, we just reflect at different times"! I said, finishing my glass.

As I talked to and observed the staff of Al Cavalluccio for the first two days I was there, I noticed that there was real diversity in their backgrounds. The team seemed to know seven languages between them.

"Are there not many Italians working here"? I asked. "Everyone seems to speak perfect or near perfect Italian".

"Most of the crew is from somewhere else", Marino told me, "but Laura is from Monfalcone. She's getting married in November. Alessandra is from here, too".

Alina was a bit of a riddle. She didn't talk to me much at first because she didn't know a word of English or German, but she had energy, rambunctiousness and resolve! She was about to clean my room once and I said to her in Italian, trying to be stern: "Don't touch my walking stick there in the corner"! Then, as I winked at her: "It's very holy and dangerous"!

"Oh, si signor Tom. Shall I polish it"? she countered, trying to be serious, yet fishing for a double-joke, both of us knowing that our language barriers might keep such jokes from developing.

Marino told me later: "Alina comes from the Ukraine. Her marriage broke up when she was only 22. She left the country with her three-year-old son and came to work in Italy. Besides, the economy was horrible there at the time".

"But her Italian seems to be fluent"! I said, astounded.

"Yes! She learned by doing, and showed great effort over the last seven years by communicating with everyone—even the lobsters! This place would fall apart without her", said Marino.

"You said that that about José, too"! I grinned.

"Yeah, but in a different way"! countered Marino.

It wasn't too busy at that moment, and Alina was giving Marino "ze evil eye" because he needed to tabulate the bills from the morning. Marino poured me a Grappa—a good one from the Collio.

"It's similar with Anna and Alessandra, he went on to explain. If Anna does not clean the place 'spic and span' at 8:00 every morning, then none of us could work! And without the charming and faithful waitressing of Alessandra the team would not be complete"!

"Did you get a chance to get to know Miroslav"? asked Marino. I had talked with Miroslav the night before, but had not known his name as I ordered my dinner. Later, he had glanced at the book I was reading, which lay on the table next to my fish. The book was from the theologian, Miroslav Volf, who had grown up in Croatia.

"That's me"! he said all of a sudden, pointing down to the table. I looked down at the picture on the cover, then over to the fish. "I'm Miroslav, too"!

"Ah! A good name", I said, catching my balance. "Are you from Croatia, like the author"?

" No, no. I'm from Serbia"!

"Yeah, he's a Serb", said Marino, as he perked up a bit, "but don't hold that against him. He can't relate to most of the attitudes shared by many in his country. He was married in Duino and has two kids. He is a good waiter, as well"!

I had a lot to think about. After meeting Luka, the quiet waiter from Slowenia and Milan, the crazy cook from Serbia, I said to Marino: "It's an international world, my friend- in this trade, more than I realized".

A WALK TO THE CROSSROADS / 113

"Do you know where I learned my English, Tom"? Marino said, winking at me as if he were getting ready to pop open some surprise. "By working as a waiter on a cruise ship between Los Angeles and Panama! During those five years I was often in your home country and spoke only with Americans".

So that's where he picked up the slight American touch, I thought. He hadn't told me that at the beginning!

I soon took off on the Rilke Path up on the ridge and let the restaurant crew work without my pestering questions. Each day I would spend two or three hours walking the path above the cliffs between Duino and Trieste. It was named after the Austrian poet and author, Rainer Maria Rilke, who spent many years, off and on, at the castle in Duino, writing and walking these very paths.

Once on the Rilke Path, I thought about the book I was reading, the one that Miroslav had discovered next to my fish. It was titled: *Exclusion and Embrace: A Theological Exploration of Identity, Otherness and Reconciliation*. The author, Miroslav Volf, was a Croatian who came from the area of Croatia, which like Bosnia survived continued acts of attrition and ethnic cleansing by the Serbian fighters, the "Cetniks", in 1993. Asking himself whether he could ever embrace one of these "Cetniks", he brings up deeper questions for all of us.

Sifting through some thoughts that were sparked by this book, I thought about the Nazi anti-aircraft gunners who were posted at various points along these cliffs during WWII. I tried to picture the young men who waited for a chance to shoot down Allied pilots who were trying to knock out the submarines in the adjoining coves and in Trieste. There they were, young German boys in a foreign country, depending on the nationalistic ideology of the Aryan-Reich to give them meaning and courage to be there, fighting, away from their families. I thought, too, of the rising nationalism in Europe in the summer and fall of 2010, when the ultra-right bolstered their arguments with anti-Islamic emotions. I also thought of the Tea Party pundits in the USA who drew fundamentalist-based patriotisms out of their holsters. It was easier than trying to think seriously about what was really best for the country's future.

I thought about the words of Miroslav concerning the Cetniks: "Such sacralisation of culture identity is invaluable for the parties in conflict because it can transmute what is in fact a murder into an act of piety. Blind to the betrayal of Christian faith that both such sacralisation of cultural identity and the atrocities it legitimizes represent, the 'holy' murderers can even see themselves as the Christian faith's valiant defenders" [weren't the crusades finished 800 years ago?] "as Serbian fighters have in their recent war against Muslims in the former Yugoslavia". He writes further: "Christian communities, which should be 'the salt' of the culture, are too often as insipid as everything around them". In thinking about the best way to be in relation to our own culture with its new "tribalism", he writes: "The answer lies, I propose, in cultivating the proper relation between distance from the culture and belonging to it".

I also thought about the team at Al Cavalluccio, coming from all parts of the world, working together. They all had gone through something, some kind of suffering. Somehow these experiences made them global citizens in a positive way. They would tend not to fall into the trap of being blind to the delusions of their own culture.

As a child from an Italian-speaking Croatian family, Marino had also suffered when he was forced out of his homeland because he spoke Italian and did not accept the ideology of Slavic communism. As a young boy, he had slept in the barracks in Trieste with thousands of Italian-speaking Croatians who had been pushed off the new Yugoslavian map. Their shelter was an old compound made from bombed-out remains of the torture chambers the Nazi SS had used during WWII.

Marino was divorced and now his second wife has cancer.

He does not drink much himself—but passes on the joy of the wine culture.

He passes on the joy of multi-cultural learning.

He passes on the joy of teamwork and simple things.

He has gone through a lot and I believe that he has transformed his pain into joy.

It flowed over everyone I met there!

It flowed all over me.

Thanks, Marino.

Thanks team!

Mille Grazie!

THE RILKE PATH

A Walk
*My eyes already touch the sunny hill,
going far ahead of the road I have begun.
So we are grasped by what we cannot grasp;
it has inner light, even from a distance—
and changes us, even if we do not reach it,
into something else, which, hardly sensing it,
we already are; a gesture waves us on
answering our own wave...
but what we feel is the wind in our faces.*

Rainer Maria Rilke, *The Collected Poems of Rainer Maria Rilke*

On the first evening in Duino, I stood naked as a jaybird in my room at Al Cavalluccio and watched the sun set over the upper Adriatic Sea. I could hear the tinkling of glasses and silverware as they mixed with the conversations on the terrace below. There were no waves in the sea and the harbour area was still.

I took my Moleskine journal and began to write a poem. I have not written many poems in my life; it always seemed too embarrassing and I was never deeply inspired to do so. But now, suddenly, it seemed a better idea to indulge my literary fantasy than to dive down onto the Viennese enjoying their lobster dinners in the restaurant below.

Sunset Over Duino
He took her smile to be something it was not
She took his smile like a hot dish, very hot
Truth was tested as they tried to be real
But words got in the way
Like broken spokes in a wheel

I had been reading through the poems of the poet Rainer Maria Rilke six months before, but I did not know that his words would lead me to visit Duino, where he created some of his most famous works. Now I found myself trekking uphill to the dramatic path that was developed in his memory.

The Rilke path is really something special. It is for observers, trekkers and poets alike. It winds from the Duino Castle on the top of the cliffs and along the upper Adriatic until it reaches the small cove at Sistiana. Rilke spent months here just writing and musing. The path was designed as a place of quiet contemplation and enjoyment for the general public.

Some of its unexpected uniqueness lies in the amazing synthesis of white rock and trees. The views southwest towards Grado and southeast towards Trieste are breathtaking. The Rilke Path also seems to bring out the poetic and meditative side in a person. I began writing prolifically after the first hour on the path! Apparently I was ready to dive into the writing mode after walking for five days.

During the first half hour of my journey, however, I was in pain. An old foot injury surfaced and I was not sure if I would have to turn back. The pain was like an old friend; I knew it well. As I kept walking, I thought of the scene in the film about Abraham that I like to show to the eleven year olds at the school where I teach religion. Towards the beginning of the movie, Terah, Abraham's father, fakes back pain ("It's like an old friend, don't worry, it's nothing, really. You two go on without me"). He does this so that his other son Nabor (the industrious and pragmatic go-getter) can have a man-to-man talk with Abe. Nabor wants to convince his brother to take a second wife and to buy some new idols that had been blessed by the local fertility gods. Nabor was giving the right advice for his time and position in his culture: "Abraham is childless. This can't go on much longer! Sarah is not bearing kids—we just have to look around for a better solution"! was Nabor's caring but pragmatic advice.

The film's interpretation strays from the biblical narrative a bit, but captures the gist of what's going on. Abraham is disappointed that he does not have children, but loves Sarah above all things. In addition, he is not satisfied with the status quo. He thinks that the fertility idols are a bunch of bullshit and senses a calling to move away from his father's household, to follow his heart, to "get real" and to take his clan somewhere else, risking everything! The beautiful part of the story is when Terah gives Abraham his blessing even though he does not completely understand him or his new calling.

As I kept walking, the sore foot got better, as is often the case when you allow blood to flow to the injured area. The Abraham story caused me to think about a lot of garbage I had been carrying around in my soul for a long time. Abraham's longing to be true to himself and his calling was appealing. I sat on a bench and wrote down a list of things I needed to look at—all sorts of "false idols"—old patterns of thinking about how life should be lived. These included playing hidden power games and pleasing others while denying my own intuition. They were things that I had partially looked at but had not changed—and they were beginning to surface. This

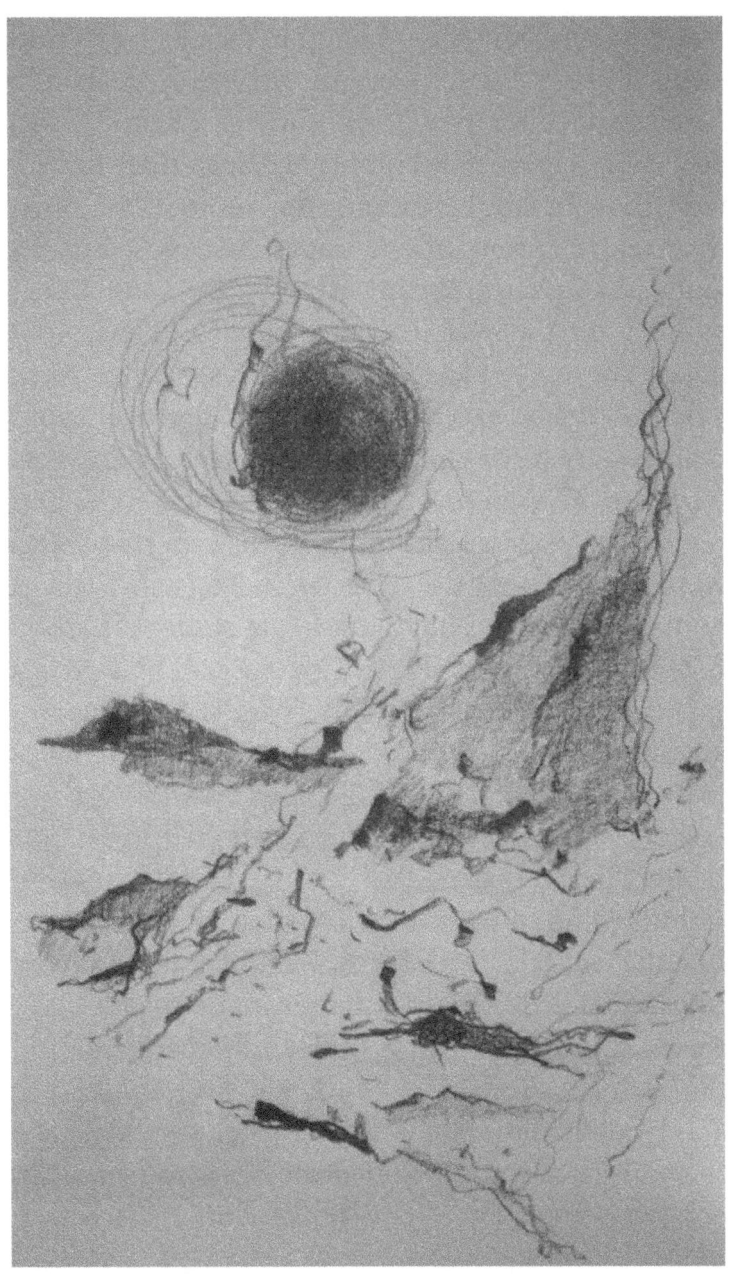

time I was naming them better; in fact, as I described them, I gave them personal names. I wanted to throw each of them over the cliffs of Duino by their ears, and I think I accomplished just that! Later, I even thought about naming this story "The Seven Drowned Demons of the upper Adriatic", but that sounded a little too theatrical.

As I let the walking stick choose choice spots among the rocky places on the grey and white stone, I passed many excellent observation points which had been used for centuries; they were moulded and worked over even more during the world wars. During WWI, the sailors of the Austrian Hungarian Monarchy sent Morse code with flags to warn of coming ships that could attack the strategic harbour in Trieste. The royal ships of the monarchy were stationed there. German WWII soldiers later manned anti-aircraft guns on these beautiful points, trying to do their best to knock off the Allied planes that tried to drop bombs on submarines stationed in Sistiana, the next harbour over.

I hiked up to one of the old lookouts and noticed that the soldiers had blasted out an underground tunnel that led underneath the lookout area. As I walked through it, I came out at a dramatic outcropping right in the middle of the cliffs. One false step and I could have fallen to the rocky cliffs below. From there one commanded the best view of all the lookout points. There I was, like a little sparrow, in the midst of giant cliffs towering above the northern shores of the Adriatic Sea!

As I stood there something happened inwardly and very quietly. I realized that I did not need to give any of those "false gods" one ounce of my power. When I embrace them as crutches and let their voices define who I am, I do not trust the treasure that is deep within me! I was reminded of words from Celtic spirituality:

> *I hear the yearnings that are in me and the fears, the hopes that rise from within and the doubts that trouble my soul. In the beginnings of this day, O God, before the night's stillness is lost to the day's busyness, open to me the treasure of my inner being that in the midst of this day's busyness I may draw on wisdom.*
> J. Phillip Newell, *Sounds of the Eternal: A Celtic Psalter*

It had taken me a long time to see how much I tend to control situations or people, although I think I am trying to better the situation. Letting people be as they are, instead of wanting to change and judge them, stems from my journey of learning to remain in my own skin—to remain on my side of the fence, as it were. It starts with me. This new view takes the weapons out of the hands of the inner accuser—real or false. "To thine own self be true", may seem like old-fashioned jargon from William Shakespeare, but it is probably the most difficult task we all have!

When being true to self, one often needs to shoot down and deny the "false gods" that constantly clamour for our attention.

At the end of the Rilke Path there is a nice café with a view down to Sistiana. Adjacent to the café is a campground. As I sat and drank a beer, I glanced below at a family camping there. I was instantly involved in their drama on the other side of the fence, inwardly criticizing how they handled their kids and how they talked to each other. *There I go again!* I said to myself.

In the next moments I didn't know whether to laugh or to cry. The Italian-pop music blared from the café, flowing over the cliffs and reminding me that even the most idyllic experiences in nature have their "boundaries and fences". Soon I would be returning to the boisterous voices and bellowing of daily life. As I looked out to sea it dawned on me that I finally understood Tom Bombadil, a character that appears in the first book of *The Lord of the Rings*. My thoughts turned back twenty years to my stay on the Island of Elba where I was doing some writing on my doctoral thesis. I was reading *Lord of the Rings* while leaning against the back of an old VW Bus in the sun, trying to figure out what on earth the Tom Bombadil story meant!

The One Ring of Power held no power over Tom Bombadil. The council in Rivendell seemed to think that he would probably forget where he placed the darn thing. One thing was sure of this oldest of all persons in Middle-earth: He stayed within his boundaries. He stayed within love. That's why he was so free and so alive. Maybe that was the reason why he heard the voices of those in need—he did not let the false voices around him have command over him. Perhaps that was why he sang so much!

Retracing my steps to Duino on the Rilke Path, I was already looking forward to diving into the ocean again and drinking wine with Marino at *Al Cavalluccio*. I mused that I never finished my doctoral work. No big loss. The stories about my walking tour were now growing in my soul. I passed the spot where I had vaulted the "seven demons" into the sea by the rear of their pants, raised my walking stick into the air and began to sing! I felt the wind caressing my skin and it whispered to me: *"Andiamo! Go for it"!*

DIFFERENT EYES

The path to the goal is the path of the hero.
The path to home is the path of love.

Gernot Candolini, Labyrinths: Walking Toward The Center

Leaving Duino turned out to be more difficult than I thought. It was somewhat of a *déjà vu* thing, once again. I almost headed off in the wrong direction as I had in Cividale nine days before. I took the wrong bus and headed toward Trieste! When I realized my mistake, I tapped the driver on the shoulder with my walking stick and asked him to let me off—and "*subito,* as soon as possible, please"! Evidently, I had been standing on the wrong side of the street! I chuckled to myself that I probably didn't want to go home just yet! The journey back through southern Friuli turned out to be a sobering and eye-opening experience—once I found the right bus.

The bus drivers were used to passengers that were confused. Duino is the home of the United World College of the Adriatic. Two hundred high school students from 80 countries gather there to study and learn to live together. I met them all over Duino; in fact, they make up a large part of the population of Duino proper! The town was chosen because of the historic conflicts between Germanic, Latin and Slavic cultures. It was intended to be an experiment in international cooperation. With all those students from all over the world, there were bound to be constant mix-ups and wrong busses taken.

My path finally turned towards home—towards Austria. Having grown up in Southern California, I was used to having people ask where "home" is. It is always a bit difficult to explain that though I consider both places home, I am now more at home in Austria with my family and close friends around me. It is equally interesting to try to explain the different perspectives one gains after living in two cultures over a long period of time. One sees things differently. It must be especially profound when a person raised in Uganda or Afghanistan moves to Salzburg or Los Angeles!

I felt something similar driving quickly past the "old stomping grounds" of my walking tour—this time on a public bus full of Italians. The bus to Udine took its time following, during the first hour, the same route I had pioneered with my walking stick. Each stop offered a small change of perspective—it went a bit too fast for me!

The first stop was in Villagio del Pescatore. The bus veered down that very hill I had decided not to explore on my way to Duino. There on my right was the harbour and the delta of the Timavo, the river that flows out of the rocks after a thirty-five-kilometre journey underground. In the village, people were doing their daily jobs. Sailboats floated on harbour waters that flowed out of a wider Timavo, with its blue-green water. Their masts bobbed back and forth, as if they were waiting for their owners to take them sailing.

I thought about the sobering part of the Timavo story. Marino had told me that the residents of Duino had been drawing water from the Timavo for hundreds of years. Since 2005, things had changed. Today the people get their drinking water solely from the Isonzo because the Timavo is slightly polluted. I was a bit shocked at first, as I had imagined that the Timavo might be the only river left that was not polluted. The truth was, however, that water quality control had not been stringent enough in the middle of Slovenia during the 1970s and 1980s. Pollution trickled down into the underground caves that supply the Timavo. The amounts were small, but the drinking water will not be safe for consumption for a long time.

I felt sad that this symbolic and beautiful natural spring had been polluted. Even now, months after my journey, I sense the strong metaphoric strength of the Timavo. It springs up out of nowhere, out of the cliffs! The Timavo then refreshes and flows in its healing capacity, to the sea.

"Good bye, for now, you faithful and humble friend"! I whispered.

The bus took us by the "crossroads" as I had named it. I saw the howling stone wolves on the outcropping and the war monuments warning us all to learn from the past. Across the road, I saw the church and its massive graveyard above me. I thought about the crossroads of Europe and the polluted Timavo flowing underneath the bus as we drove quickly over it. There are very few signs pointing tourists to the Timavo source. Perhaps it was better that way.

Then we neared the "Il Duce" railroad bridge, as I called it, and arrived in Monfalcone much sooner than I could have on foot. The shipbuilding town looked beautiful in the late morning sun. The bus passed the place where Francesco and I bought our ice cream and had our talks. Weary workers climbed into the bus after working the night shift. Mothers with small children climbed in on their way to visit Grandma in Udine, the main city in Friuli. I said a prayer for the marriage of Laura, as well as for Francesco, the "soft-hearted-macho". I even took a peak out the back window of the bus to see where the Karst started along the ridge, trying to spot the back road Francesco had taken on our midnight journey to the signora's house.

Carted through the towns and countryside in that bus, I felt as if I had lost power, my relationship to nature diminishing as I rushed back into the fast-moving traffic mode. I no longer experienced each meter as an "adventure in feeling with different eyes" and yet, in spite of my sober feelings, it was invigorating reflecting on the unique happenings of the past few days.

We moved into a new century when we hit the airport, the next stop. I hadn't even known that there was an airport between Monfalcone and Grado—the planes must have a "whisper jet" planted in their bodies! It was plain as day that this was the new "crossroads" of the area. To get to Grado, Trieste, or Friuli and Slovenia fast—fly into this airport! The planes fly over these "crossroads", while the Timavo continues to flow, surely unrecognized by the jetsetters above. Maybe there will always be some crazy foot travellers with walking sticks down there, gathering new perspectives!

Just a few minutes after leaving the airport, we finally crossed the Isonzo River! Here it became very large, just before merging with the Torre, which flows down from Udine and the Italian Alps, this side of Austria. The Natisone flows into the heart of the Torre River a few kilometres to the north. The bus promptly crossed the Torre, too! The weather had changed; it was overcast and a light rain was falling, mirroring the feeling I had that I was very glad I had not taken this route. A well-known natural reserve on the delta of the Isonzo begins two kilometres downstream with its acres of reeds and long grass, teeming with thousands of birds. This time, however, I was glad for the different eyes I gained by

A WALK TO THE CROSSROADS / 133

heading for Duino instead—and for meeting those crazy "birds" at *Al Cavalluccio!*

Suddenly, we were crossing an inland plateau on the way to Palmanova and then on to Udine. As I looked northeast I saw, clearly and simply, as if it were my second home, a hilly region full of memories—the Collio! I saw it from the south, "from a distance", as in Bette Midler's song. The sky was overcast, but it was fun to recognize this extraordinary wine region like an old friend, just ten kilometres away. I had been up it, through it, into it, around it and below it! Cormons lay like a small jewel at its base. From a distance, it seemed so simple for Italians to get along with Slovenians, to offer good prices for good wine. From a distance, things always look rosy!

In any case, one thing is sure: This adventure gave me different eyes! Writing such things could seem a bit clichéd, but it's true. Over the months I have increasingly noticed the birds around me. I sit and watch more. I take walks with my walking stick through the outskirts of the city and plan pockets in my days to discover new areas. The strong walking stick grounds me and I remain within my personal "boundaries" more often, gaining respect for the voices of others!

I'm deeply thankful for the many people who crossed my path during these days and enriched my life. My family thought I was bit crazy, but they gave me their blessing.

One thing is clear: It takes a decision to do it!

See you sometime—on a walking tour!

ACKNOWLEDGEMENTS

Chapter 1: Prologue to adventure
Tolkien, JRR, *The Lord of the Rings, Book I*. Harper Collins Publishers, 1991.

Chapter 2: Submarines in Italy
Newby, Eric, *Love and War in the Apennines*. London: Lonely Planet Publishers, 2008.
Tournier, Paul, *The Adventure Of Living*. New York: Harper and Row Publishers, 1965.

Chapter 3: Detours and Disney
Candolini, Gernot, *Labyrinths: Walking Toward the Center*. New York: Crossroad Publishing Company, 2003.

Chapter 4: The Red Rooster
Candolini, Gernot, *Labyrinths: Walking Toward the Center*. New York: Crossroad Publishing Company, 2003.

Chapter 5: The Old Road
Tolkien, JRR, *The Lord of the Rings, Book I*. London: Harper Collins Publishers, 1991.

Chapter 6: Francesco
Lewis, C.S., *Perelandra*. New York: Macmillan Publishing Co., 1944.

Chapter 7: Timavo at the Crossroads
Isaiah 48:6, Old Testament, New English Bible. Oxford: Bible Society, 1990.

Chapter 8: Al Cavalluccio
Candolini, Gernot, *Labyrinths: Walking Toward the Center*. New York: Crossroad Publishing Company, 2003
Volf, Miroslav, *Exclusion & Embrace*. Nashville, TN: Abingdon Press, 1996.
The photo on page 104 was taken by my son, Michael, a month after my tour. It was taken from Duino Castle looking towards the old castle-ruins, with Monfalcone in the background. Just over the rim is the swimming area and Duino to the right. The water we see is the Timavo flowing into the Adriatic.

Chapter 9: The Rilke Path
Rilke, Rainer Maria, Collected Poems of Rainer Maria Rilke: A Translation from the German and Commentary by Robert Bly (Robert Bly, translator). New York: Harper Perennial Publishers, 1981.
Newell, J.Phillip, *Sounds of the Eternal, A Celtic Psalter*. Grand Rapids, MI: William B. Eerdmans Publishing Company, 2002.

Chapter 10: Different Eyes
Candolini, Gernot, *Labyrinths: Walking Toward the Center*. New York: Crossroad Publishing Company, 2003.

www.ingramcontent.com/pod-product-compliance
Lightning Source LLC
Chambersburg PA
CBHW020939090426
42736CB00010B/1193